A
THEOLOGICO-POLITICAL
TREATISE

PART II
CHAPTERS VI TO X

A
THEOLOGICO-POLITICAL
TREATISE

PART II
CHAPTERS VI TO X

By
BENEDICT DE SPINOZA

Also known as
BARUCH SPINOZA

ARC
MANOR
ROCKVILLE, MARYLAND
2008

ISBN: 978-1-60450-214-5

Published by Arc Manor
P. O. Box 10339
Rockville, MD 20849-0339
www.ArcManor.com

Printed in the United States of America/United Kingdom

Contents

CHAPTER VI

Of Miracles

As men are accustomed to call Divine the knowledge which transcends human understanding, so also do they style Divine, or the work of God, anything of which the cause is not generally known: for the masses think that the power and providence of God are most clearly displayed by events that are extraordinary and contrary to the conception they have formed of nature, especially if such events bring them any profit or convenience: they think that the clearest possible proof of God's existence is afforded when nature, as they suppose, breaks her accustomed order, and consequently they believe that those who explain or endeavour to understand phenomena or miracles through their natural causes are doing away with God and His providence. They suppose, forsooth, that God is inactive so long as nature works in her accustomed order, and vice versa, that the power of nature and natural causes are idle so long as God is acting: thus they imagine two powers distinct one from the other, the power of God and the power of nature, though the latter is in a sense determined by God, or (as most people believe now) created by Him. What they mean by either, and what they understand by God and nature they do not know, except that they imagine the power of God to be like that of some royal potentate, and nature's power to consist in force and energy.

The masses then style unusual phenomena, "miracles," and partly from piety, partly for the sake of opposing the students of science, prefer to remain in ignorance of natural causes, and only to hear of those things which they know least, and consequently admire most. In fact, the common people can only adore God, and refer all things to His power by removing natural causes, and conceiving things happening out of their due course, and only admires the power of God when the power of nature is conceived of as in subjection to it.

This idea seems to have taken its rise among the early Jews who saw the Gentiles round them worshipping visible gods such as the sun, the moon, the earth, water, air, &c., and in order to inspire the conviction that such divinities were weak and inconstant, or changeable, told how they themselves were under the sway of an invisible God, and narrated their miracles, trying further to show that the God whom they worshipped arranged the whole of nature for their sole benefit: this idea was so pleasing to humanity that men go on to this day imagining miracles, so that they may believe themselves God's favourites, and the final cause for which God created and directs all things.

What pretension will not people in their folly advance! They have no single sound idea concerning either God or nature, they confound God's decrees with human decrees, they conceive nature as so limited that they believe man to be its chief part! I have spent enough space in setting forth these common ideas and prejudices concerning nature and miracles, but in order to afford a regular demonstration I will show—

I. That nature cannot be contravened, but that she preserves a fixed and immutable order, and at the same time I will explain what is meant by a miracle.

II. That God's nature and existence, and consequently His providence cannot be known from miracles, but that they can all be much better perceived from the fixed and immutable order of nature.

III. That by the decrees and volitions, and consequently the providence of God, Scripture (as I will prove by Scriptural examples) means nothing but nature's order following necessarily from her eternal laws.

IV. Lastly, I will treat of the method of interpreting Scriptural miracles, and the chief points to be noted concerning the narratives of them.

Such are the principal subjects which will be discussed in this chapter, and which will serve, I think, not a little to further the object of this treatise.

Our first point is easily proved from what we showed in Chap. IV. about Divine law—namely, that all that God wishes or determines involves eternal necessity, and truth, for we demonstrated that God's understanding is identical with His will, and that it is the same thing to say that God wills a thing, as to say, that He understands it; hence, as it follows necessarily, from the Divine nature and perfection that God understands a thing as it is, it follows no less necessarily that He wills it as it is. Now, as nothing is necessarily true save only by, Divine decree, it is plain that the universal laws of nature are decrees of God following from the necessity and perfection of the Divine nature. Hence, any event happening in nature which contravened nature's universal laws, would necessarily also contravene the Divine decree, nature, and understanding; or if anyone asserted that God acts in contravention to the laws of nature, he, ipso facto, would be compelled to assert that God acted against His own nature—an evident absurdity. One might easily show from the same premises that the power and efficiency, of nature are in themselves the Divine power and efficiency, and that the Divine power is the very essence of God, but this I gladly pass over for the present.

Nothing, then, comes to pass in nature (N.B. I do not mean here by "nature," merely matter and its modifications, but infinite other things besides matter.) in contravention to her universal laws, nay, everything agrees with them and follows from them, for whatsoever comes to pass, comes to pass by the will and eternal decree of God; that is, as we have just pointed out, whatever comes to pass, comes to pass according to laws and rules which involve eternal necessity and truth; nature, therefore, always observes laws and rules which involve eternal necessity, and truth, although they may not all

9

be known to us, and therefore she keeps a fixed and mutable order. Nor is there any sound reason for limiting the power and efficacy of nature, and asserting that her laws are fit for certain purposes, but not for all; for as the efficacy, and power of nature, are the very, efficacy and power of God, and as the laws and rules of nature are the decrees of God, it is in every way to be believed that the power of nature is infinite, and that her laws are broad enough to embrace everything conceived by, the Divine intellect; the only alternative is to assert that God has created nature so weak, and has ordained for her laws so barren, that He is repeatedly compelled to come afresh to her aid if He wishes that she should be preserved, and that things should happen as He desires: a conclusion, in My opinion, very far removed from reason. Further, as nothing happens in nature which does not follow from her laws, and as her laws embrace everything conceived by the Divine intellect, and lastly, as nature preserves a fixed and immutable order; it most clearly follows that miracles are only intelligible as in relation to human opinions, and merely mean events of which the natural cause cannot be explained by a reference to any ordinary occurrence, either by us, or at any rate, by the writer and narrator of the miracle.

We may, in fact, say that a miracle is an event of which the causes annot be explained by the natural reason through a reference to ascertained workings of nature; but since miracles were wrought according to the understanding of the masses, who are wholly ignorant of the workings of nature, it is certain that the ancients took for a miracle whatever they could not explain by the method adopted by the unlearned in such cases, namely, an appeal to the memory, a recalling of something similar, which is ordinarily regarded without wonder; for most people think they sufficiently understand a thing when they have ceased to wonder at it. The ancients, then, and indeed most men up to the present day, had no other criterion for a miracle; hence we cannot doubt that many things are narrated in Scripture as miracles of which the causes could easily be explained by reference to ascertained workings of nature. We have hinted as much in Chap. ii., in speaking of the sun standing still in the time of Joshua, and to say on the subject when we come to treat of the interpretation of miracles later on in this chapter.

It is now time to pass on to the second point, and show that we cannot gain an understanding of God's essence, existence, or providence by means of miracles, but that these truths are much better perceived through the fixed and immutable order of nature. I thus proceed with the demonstration. As God's existence is not self-evident[1] it must necessarily be inferred from ideas so firmly and incontrovertibly true, that no power can be postulated or conceived sufficient to impugn them. They ought certainly so to appear to us when we infer from them God's existence, if we wish to place our conclusion beyond the reach of doubt; for if we could conceive that such ideas could be impugned by any power whatsoever, we should doubt of their truth, we should doubt of our conclusion, namely, of God's existence, and should never be able to be certain of anything. Further, we know that nothing either agrees with or is contrary to nature, unless it agrees with or is contrary to these primary ideas; wherefore if we would conceive that anything could be done in nature by any power whatsoever which would be contrary to the laws of nature, it would also be contrary to our primary ideas, and we should have either to reject it as absurd, or else to cast doubt (as just shown) on our primary ideas, and consequently on the existence of God, and on everything howsoever perceived. Therefore miracles, in the sense of events contrary to the laws of nature, so far from demonstrating to us the existence of God, would, on the contrary, lead us to doubt it, where, otherwise, we might have been absolutely certain of it, as knowing that nature follows a fixed and immutable order.

Let us take miracle as meaning that which cannot be explained through natural causes. This may be interpreted in two senses: either as that which has natural causes, but cannot be examined by the human intellect; or as that which has no cause save God and God's will. But as all things which come to pass through natural causes, come to pass

---

1   See Endnote 6.

also solely through the will and power of God, it comes to this, that a miracle, whether it has natural causes or not, is a result which cannot be explained by its cause, that is a phenomenon which surpasses human understanding; but from such a phenomenon, and certainly from a result surpassing our understanding, we can gain no knowledge. For whatsoever we understand clearly and distinctly should be plain to us either in itself or by means of something else clearly and distinctly understood; wherefore from a miracle or a phenomenon which we cannot understand, we can gain no knowledge of God's essence, or existence, or indeed anything about God or nature; whereas when we know that all things are ordained and ratified by God, that the operations of nature follow from the essence of God, and that the laws of nature are eternal decrees and volitions of God, we must perforce conclude that our knowledge of God, and of God's will increases in proportion to our knowledge and clear understanding of nature, as we see how she depends on her primal cause, and how she works according to eternal law. Wherefore so far as our understanding goes, those phenomena which we clearly and distinctly understand have much better right to be called works of God, and to be referred to the will of God than those about which we are entirely ignorant, although they appeal powerfully to the imagination, and compel men's admiration.

It is only phenomena that we clearly and distinctly understand, which heighten our knowledge of God, and most clearly indicate His will and decrees. Plainly, they are but triflers who, when they cannot explain a thing, run back to the will of God; this is, truly, a ridiculous way of expressing ignorance. Again, even supposing that some conclusion could be drawn from miracles, we could not possibly infer from them the existence of God: for a miracle being an event under limitations is the expression of a fixed and limited power; therefore we could not possibly infer from an effect of this kind the existence of a cause whose power is infinite, but at the utmost only of a cause whose power is greater than that of the said effect. I say at the utmost, for a phenomenon may be the result of many concurrent causes, and its power may be less than the power of the sum of such causes, but far greater than that of any one of them taken individually. On the other hand, the laws of nature, as we have shown, extend over infinity, and are conceived by us as, after a fashion, eternal, and nature works in accordance with them in a fixed and immutable order; therefore, such laws indicate to us in a certain degree the infinity, the eternity, and the immutability of God.

We may conclude, then, that we cannot gain knowledge of the existence and providence of God by means of miracles, but that we can far better infer them from the fixed and immutable order of nature. By miracle, I here mean an event which surpasses, or is thought to surpass, human comprehension: for in so far as it is supposed to destroy or interrupt the order of nature or her laws, it not only can give us no knowledge of God, but, contrariwise, takes away that which we naturally have, and makes us doubt of God and everything else.

Neither do I recognize any difference between an event against the laws of nature and an event beyond the laws of nature (that is, according to some, an event which does not contravene nature, though she is inadequate to produce or effect it)—for a miracle is wrought in, and not beyond nature, though it may be said in itself to be above nature, and, therefore, must necessarily interrupt the order of nature, which otherwise we conceive of as fixed and unchangeable, according to God's decrees. If, therefore, anything should come to pass in nature which does not follow from her laws, it would also be in contravention to the order which God has established in nature for ever through universal natural laws: it would, therefore, be in contravention to God's nature and laws, and, consequently, belief in it would throw doubt upon everything, and lead to Atheism.

I think I have now sufficiently established my second point, so that we can again conclude that a miracle, whether in contravention to, or beyond, nature, is a mere absurdity; and, therefore, that what is meant in Scripture by a miracle can only be a work of nature, which surpasses, or is believed to surpass, human comprehension. Before passing on to my third point, I will adduce Scriptural authority for my assertion that God cannot be known from miracles. Scripture nowhere states the doctrine openly, but it can readily be inferred from several passages. Firstly, that in which Moses commands (Deut. xiii.) that a false prophet should be put to death, even though he work miracles: "If there arise a prophet among you, and giveth thee a sign or wonder, and the sign or wonder come to pass, saying, Let us go after other gods . . . thou shalt not hearken unto the voice of that prophet; for the Lord your God proveth you, and that prophet shall be put to death." From this it clearly follows that miracles could be wrought even by false prophets; and that, unless men are honestly endowed with the true knowledge and love of God, they may be as easily led by miracles to follow false gods as to follow the true God; for these words are added: "For the Lord your God tempts you, that He may know whether you love Him with all your heart and with all your mind."

Further, the Israelites, from all their miracles, were unable to form a sound conception of God, as their experience testified: for when they had persuaded themselves that Moses had departed from among them, they petitioned Aaron to give them visible gods; and the idea of God they had formed as the result of all their miracles was—a calf!

Asaph, though he had heard of so many miracles, yet doubted of the providence of God, and would have turned himself from the true way, if he had not at last come to understand true blessedness. (See Ps. lxxxiii.) Solomon, too, at a time when the Jewish nation was at the height of its prosperity, suspects that all things happen by chance. (See Eccles. iii:19, 20, 21; and chap. ix:2, 3, &c.)

Lastly, nearly all the prophets found it very hard to reconcile the order of nature and human affairs with the conception they had formed of God's providence, whereas philosophers who endeavour to understand things by clear conceptions of them, rather than by miracles, have always found the task extremely easy—at least, such of them as place true happiness solely in virtue and peace of mind, and who aim at obeying nature, rather than being obeyed by her. Such persons rest assured that God directs nature according to the requirements of universal laws, not according to the requirements of the particular laws of human nature, and trial, therefore, God's scheme comprehends, not only the human race, but the whole of nature.

It is plain, then, from Scripture itself, that miracles can give no knowledge of God, nor clearly teach us the providence of God. As to the frequent statements in Scripture, that God wrought miracles to make Himself plain to man—as in Exodus x:2, where He deceived the Egyptians, and gave signs of Himself, that the Israelites might know that He was God,—it does not, therefore, follow that miracles really taught this truth, but only that the Jews held opinions which laid them easily open to conviction by miracles. We have shown in Chap. II. that the reasons assigned by the prophets, or those which are formed from revelation, are not assigned in accordance with ideas universal and common to all, but in accordance with the accepted doctrines, however absurd, and with the opinions of those to whom the revelation was given, or those whom the Holy Spirit wished to convince.

This we have illustrated by many Scriptural instances, and can further cite Paul, who to the Greeks was a Greek, and to the Jews a Jew. But although these miracles could convince the Egyptians and Jews from their standpoint, they could not give a true idea and knowledge of God, but only cause them to admit that there was a Deity more powerful than anything known to them, and that this Deity took special care of the Jews, who had just then an unexpectedly happy issue of all their affairs. They could not teach them that God cares equally for all, for this can be taught only by philosophy: the Jews, and all who took their knowledge of God's providence from the dissimilarity of human conditions of life and the inequalities of fortune, persuaded themselves that God loved the Jews above all men, though they did not surpass their fellows in true human perfection.

I now go on to my third point, and show from Scripture that the decrees and mandates of God, and consequently His providence, are merely the order of nature—that is, when Scripture describes an event as accomplished by God or God's will, we must understand merely that it was in accordance with the law and order of nature, not, as most people believe, that nature had for a season ceased to act, or that her order was temporarily interrupted. But Scripture does not directly teach matters unconnected with its doctrine, wherefore it has no care to explain things by their natural causes, nor to expound matters merely speculative. Wherefore our conclusion must be gathered by inference from those Scriptural narratives which happen to be written more at length and circumstantially than usual. Of these I will cite a few.

In the first book of Samuel, ix:15, 16, it is related that God revealed to Samuel that He would send Saul to him, yet God did not send Saul to Samuel as people are wont to send one man to another. His "sending" was merely the ordinary course of nature. Saul was looking for the asses he had lost, and was meditating a return home without them, when, at the suggestion of his servant, he went to the prophet Samuel, to learn from him where he might find them. From no part of the narrative does it appear that Saul had any command from God to visit Samuel beyond this natural motive.

In Psalm cv. 24 it is said that God changed the hearts of the Egyptians, so that they hated the Israelites. This was evidently a natural change, as appears from Exodus, chap.i., where we find no slight reason for the Egyptians reducing the Israelites to slavery.

In Genesis ix:13, God tells Noah that He will set His bow in the cloud; this action of God's is but another way of expressing the refraction and reflection which the rays of the sun are subjected to in drops of water.

In Psalm cxlvii:18, the natural action and warmth of the wind, by which hoar frost and snow are melted, are styled the word of the Lord, and in verse 15 wind and cold are called the commandment and word of God.

In Psalm civ:4, wind and fire are called the angels and ministers of God, and various other passages of the same sort are found in Scripture, clearly showing that the decree, commandment, fiat, and word of God are merely expressions for the action and order of nature.

Thus it is plain that all the events narrated in Scripture came to pass naturally, and are referred directly to God because Scripture, as we have shown, does not aim at explaining things by their natural causes, but only at narrating what appeals to the popular imagination, and doing so in the manner best calculated to excite wonder, and consequently to impress the minds of the masses with devotion. If, therefore, events are found in the Bible which we cannot refer to their causes, nay, which seem entirely to contradict the order of nature, we must not come to a stand, but assuredly believe that whatever did really happen happened naturally. This view is confirmed by the fact that in the case of every miracle there were many attendant circumstances, though these were not always related, especially where the narrative was of a poetic character.

The circumstances of the miracles clearly show, I maintain, that natural causes were needed. For instance, in order to infect the Egyptians with blains, it was necessary that Moses should scatter ashes in the air (Exod. ix: 10); the locusts also came upon the land of Egypt by a command of God in accordance with nature, namely, by an east wind blowing for a whole day and night; and they departed by a very strong west wind (Exod. x:14, 19). By a similar Divine mandate the sea opened a way for the Jews (Exo. xiv:21), namely, by an east wind which blew very strongly all night.

So, too, when Elisha would revive the boy who was believed to be dead, he was obliged to bend over him several times until the flesh of the child waxed warm, and at last he opened his eyes (2 Kings iv:34, 35).

Again, in John's Gospel (chap. ix.) certain acts are mentioned as performed by Christ preparatory to healing the blind man, and there are numerous other instances showing that something further than the absolute fiat of God is required for working a miracle.

Wherefore we may believe that, although the circumstances attending miracles are not related always or in full detail, yet a miracle was never performed without them.

This is confirmed by Exodus xiv:27, where it is simply stated that "Moses stretched forth his hand, and the waters of the sea returned to their strength in the morning," no mention being made of a wind; but in the song of Moses (Exod. xv:10) we read, "Thou didst blow with Thy wind (i.e. with a very strong wind), and the sea covered them." Thus the attendant circumstance is omitted in the history, and the miracle is thereby enhanced.

But perhaps someone will insist that we find many things in Scripture which seem in nowise explicable by natural causes, as for instance, that the sins of men and their prayers can be the cause of rain and of the earth's fertility, or that faith can heal the blind, and so on. But I think I have already made sufficient answer: I have shown that Scripture does not explain things by their secondary causes, but only narrates them in the order and the style which has most power to move men, and especially uneducated men, to devotion; and therefore it speaks inaccurately of God and of events, seeing that its object is not to convince the reason, but to attract and lay hold of the imagination. If the Bible were to describe the destruction of an empire in the style of political historians, the masses would remain unstirred, whereas the contrary is the case when it adopts the method of poetic description, and refers all things immediately to God. When, therefore, the Bible says that the earth is barren because of men's sins, or that the blind were healed by faith, we ought to take no more notice than when it says that God is angry at men's sins, that He is sad, that He repents of the good He has promised and done; or that on seeing a sign he remembers something He had promised, and other similar expressions, which are either thrown out poetically or related according to the opinion and prejudices of the writer.

We may, then, be absolutely certain that every event which is truly described in Scripture necessarily happened, like everything else, according to natural laws; and if anything is there set down which can be proved in set terms to contravene the order of nature, or not to be deducible therefrom, we must believe it to have been foisted into the sacred writings by irreligious hands; for whatsoever is contrary to nature is also contrary to reason, and whatsoever is contrary to reason is absurd, and, ipso facto, to be rejected.

There remain some points concerning the interpretation of miracles to be noted, or rather to be recapitulated, for most of them have been already stated. These I proceed to discuss in the fourth division of my subject, and I am led to do so lest anyone should, by wrongly interpreting a miracle, rashly suspect that he has found something in Scripture contrary to human reason.

It is very rare for men to relate an event simply as it happened, without adding any element of their own judgment. When they see or hear anything new, they are, unless strictly on their guard, so occupied with their own preconceived opinions that they perceive something quite different from the plain facts seen or heard, especially if such facts surpass the comprehension of the beholder or hearer, and, most of all, if he is interested in their happening in a given way.

Thus men relate in chronicles and histories their own opinions rather than actual events, so that one and the same event is so differently related by two men of different opinions, that it seems like two separate occurrences; and, further, it is very easy from historical chronicles to gather the personal opinions of the historian.

I could cite many instances in proof of this from the writings both of natural philosophers and historians, but I will content myself with one only from Scripture, and leave the reader to judge of the rest.

In the time of Joshua the Hebrews held the ordinary opinion that the sun moves with a daily motion, and that the earth remains at rest; to this preconceived opinion they adapted the miracle which occurred during their battle with the five kings. They did not simply relate that that day was longer than usual, but asserted that the sun and moon stood still, or ceased from their motion—a statement which would be of great service to them at that time in convincing and proving by experience to the Gentiles, who worshipped the sun, that the sun was under the control of another deity who could compel it to change its daily course. Thus, partly through religious motives, partly through preconceived opinions, they conceived of and related the occurrence as something quite different from what really happened.

Thus in order to interpret the Scriptural miracles and understand from the narration of them how they really happened, it is necessary to know the opinions of those who first related them, and have recorded them for us in writing, and to distinguish such opinions from the actual impression made upon their senses, otherwise we shall confound opinions and judgments with the actual miracle as it really occurred: nay, further, we shall confound actual events with symbolical and imaginary ones. For many things are narrated in Scripture as real, and were believed to be real, which were in fact only symbolical and imaginary. As, for instance, that God came down from heaven (Exod. xix:28, Deut. v:28), and that Mount Sinai smoked because God descended upon it surrounded with fire; or, again that Elijah ascended into heaven in a chariot of fire, with horses of fire; all these things were assuredly merely symbols adapted to the opinions of those who have handed them down to us as they were represented to them, namely, as real. All who have any education know that God has no right hand nor left; that He is not moved nor at rest, nor in a particular place, but that He is absolutely infinite and contains in Himself all perfections.

These things, I repeat, are known to whoever judges of things by the perception of pure reason, and not according as his imagination is affected by his outward senses. Following the example of the masses who imagine a bodily Deity, holding a royal court with a throne on the convexity of heaven, above the stars, which are believed to be not very, far off from the earth.

To these and similar opinions very many narrations in Scripture are adapted, and should not, therefore, be mistaken by philosophers for realities.

Lastly, in order to understand, in the case of miracles, what actually took place, we ought to be familiar with Jewish phrases and metaphors; anyone who did not make sufficient allowance for these, would be continually seeing miracles in Scripture where nothing of the kind is intended by the writer; he would thus miss the knowledge not only of what actually happened, but also of the mind of the writers of the sacred text. For instance, Zechariah speaking of some future war says (chap. xiv;7): "It shall be one day which shall be known to the Lord, not day, nor night; but at even time it shall be light." In these words he seems to predict a great miracle, yet he only means that the battle will be doubtful the whole day, that the issue will be known only to God, but that in the evening they will gain the victory: the prophets frequently used to predict victories and defeats of the nations in similar phrases. Thus Isaiah, describing the destruction of Babylon, says (chap. xiii.): "The stars of heaven, and the constellations thereof, shall not give their light; the sun shall be darkened in his going forth, and the moon shall not cause her light to shine." Now I suppose no one imagines that at the destruction of Babylon these phenomena actually occurred any more than that which the prophet adds, "For I will make the heavens to tremble, and remove the earth out of her place."

So, too, Isaiah in foretelling to the Jews that they would return from Babylon to Jerusalem in safety, and would not suffer from thirst on their journey, says: "And they thirsted not when He led them through the deserts; He caused the waters to flow out of the rocks for them; He clave the rocks, and the waters gushed out." These words merely mean that the Jews, like other people, found springs in the desert, at which they quenched their thirst; for when the Jews returned to Jerusalem with the consent of Cyrus, it is admitted that no similar miracles befell them.

In this way many occurrences in the Bible are to be regarded merely as Jewish expressions. There is no need for me to go through them in detail; but I will call attention generally to the fact that the Jews employed such phrases not only rhetorically, but also, and indeed chiefly, from devotional motives. Such is the reason for the substitution of "bless God" for "curse God" in 1 Kings xxi:10, and Job ii:9, and for all things being referred to God, whence it appears that the Bible seems to relate nothing but miracles, even when speaking of the most ordinary occurrences, as in the examples given above.

Hence we must believe that when the Bible says that the Lord hardened Pharaoh's heart, it only means that Pharaoh was obstinate; when it says that God opened the windows of heaven, it only means that it rained very hard, and so on. When we reflect on these peculiarities, and also on the fact that most things are related very shortly, with very little details and almost in abridgments, we shall see that there is hardly anything in Scripture which can be proved contrary to natural reason, while, on the other hand, many things which before seemed obscure, will after a little consideration be understood and easily explained.

I think I have now very clearly explained all that I proposed to explain, but before I finish this chapter I would call attention to the fact that I have adopted a different method in speaking of miracles to that which I employed in treating of prophecy. Of prophecy I have asserted nothing which could not be inferred from promises revealed in Scripture, whereas in this chapter I have deduced my conclusions solely from the principles ascertained by the natural light of reason. I have proceeded in this way advisedly, for prophecy, in that it surpasses human knowledge, is a purely theological question; therefore, I knew that I could not make any assertions about it, nor learn wherein it consists, except through deductions from premises that have been revealed; therefore I was compelled to collate the history of prophecy, and to draw therefrom certain conclusions which would teach me, in so far as such teaching is possible, the nature and properties of the gift. But in the case of miracles, as our inquiry is a question purely philosophical (namely, whether anything can happen which contravenes or does not follow from the laws of nature), I was not under any such necessity: I therefore thought it wiser to unravel the difficulty through premises ascertained and thoroughly known by could also easily have solved the problem merely from the doctrines and fundamental principles of Scripture: in order that everyone may acknowledge this, I will briefly show how it could be done.

Scripture makes the general assertion in several passages that nature's course is fixed and unchangeable. In Ps. cxlviii:6, for instance, and Jer. xxxi:35. The wise man also, in Eccles. i:10, distinctly teaches that "there is nothing new under the sun," and in verses 11, 12, illustrating the same idea, he adds that although something occasionally happens which seems new, it is not really new, but "hath been already of old time, which was before us, whereof there is no remembrance, neither shall there be any remembrance of things that are to come with those that come after." Again in chap. iii:11, he says, "God hath made everything beautiful in his time," and immediately afterwards adds, "I know that whatsoever God doeth, it shall be for ever; nothing can be put to it, nor anything taken from it."

Now all these texts teach most distinctly that nature preserves a fixed and unchangeable order, and that God in all ages, known and unknown, has been the same; further, that the laws of nature are so perfect, that nothing can be added thereto nor taken therefrom; and, lastly, that miracles only appear as something new because of man's ignorance.

Such is the express teaching of Scripture: nowhere does Scripture assert that anything happens which contradicts, or cannot follow from the laws of nature; and, therefore, we should not attribute to it such a doctrine.

To these considerations we must add, that miracles require causes and attendant circumstances, and that they follow, not from some mysterious royal power which the masses attribute to God, but from the Divine rule and decree, that is (as we have shown from Scripture itself) from the laws and order of nature; lastly, that miracles can be wrought even by false prophets, as is proved from Deut. xiii. and Matt. xxiv:24.

The conclusion, then, that is most plainly put before us is, that miracles were natural occurrences, and must therefore be so explained as to appear neither new (in the words of Solomon) nor contrary to nature, but, as far as possible, in complete agreement with ordinary events. This can easily be done by anyone, now that I have set forth the rules drawn from Scripture. Nevertheless, though I maintain that Scripture teaches this doctrine, I do not assert that it teaches it as a truth necessary to salvation, but only that the prophets were in agreement with ourselves on the point; therefore everyone is free to think on the subject as he likes, according as he thinks it best for himself, and most likely to conduce to the worship of God and to singlehearted religion.

This is also the opinion of Josephus, for at the conclusion of the second book of his "Antiquities," he writes: Let no man think this story incredible of the sea's dividing to save these people, for we find it in ancient records that this hath been seen before, whether by God's extraordinary will or by the course of nature it is indifferent. The same thing happened one time to the Macedonians, under the command of Alexander, when for want of another passage the Pamphylian Sea divided to make them way; God's Providence making use of Alexander at that time as His instrument for destroying the Persian Empire. This is attested by all the historians who have pretended to write the Life of that Prince. But people are at liberty to think what they please."

Such are the words of Josephus, and such is his opinion on faith in miracles.

CHAPTER VII

Of the Interpretation of Scripture

WHEN people declare, as all are ready, to do, that the Bible is the Word of God teaching man true blessedness and the way of salvation, they evidently do not mean what they, say; for the masses take no pains at all to live according to Scripture, and we see most people endeavouring to hawk about their own commentaries as the word of God, and giving their best efforts, under the guise of religion, to compelling others to think as they do: we generally see, I say, theologians anxious to learn how to wring their inventions and sayings out of the sacred text, and to fortify, them with Divine authority. Such persons never display, less scruple or more zeal than when they, are interpreting Scripture or the mind of the Holy Ghost; if we ever see them perturbed, it is not that they fear to attribute some error to the Holy Spirit, and to stray from the right path, but that they are afraid to be convicted of error by, others, and thus to overthrow and bring into contempt their own authority. But if men really believed what they verbally testify of Scripture, they would adopt quite a different plan of life: their minds would not be agitated by so many contentions, nor so many hatreds, and they would cease to be excited by such a blind and rash passion for interpreting the sacred writings, and excogitating novelties in religion. On the contrary, they would not dare to adopt, as the teaching of Scripture, anything which they could not plainly deduce therefrom: lastly, those sacrilegious persons who have dared, in several passages, to interpolate the Bible, would have shrunk from so great a crime, and would have stayed their sacrilegious hands.

Ambition and unscrupulousness have waxed so powerful, that religion is thought to consist, not so much in respecting the writings of the Holy Ghost, as in defending human commentaries, so that religion is no longer identified with charity, but with spreading discord and propagating insensate hatred disguised under the name of zeal for the Lord, and eager ardour.

To these evils we must add superstition, which teaches men to despise reason and nature, and only to admire and venerate that which is repugnant to both: whence it is not wonderful that for the sake of increasing the admiration and veneration felt for Scripture, men strive to explain it so as to make it appear to contradict, as far as possible, both one and the other: thus they dream that most profound mysteries lie hid in the Bible, and weary themselves out in the investigation of these absurdities, to the neglect of what is useful. Every result of their diseased imagination they attribute to the Holy Ghost, and strive to defend with the utmost zeal and passion; for it is an observed fact that men employ their reason to defend conclusions arrived at by reason, but conclusions arrived at by the passions are defended by the passions.

If we would separate ourselves from the crowd and escape from theological prejudices, instead of rashly accepting human commentaries for Divine documents, we must consider the true method of interpreting Scripture and dwell upon it at some length: for if we remain in ignorance of this we cannot know, certainly, what the Bible and the Holy Spirit wish to teach.

I may sum up the matter by saying that the method of interpreting Scripture does not widely differ from the method of interpreting nature—in fact, it is almost the same. For as the interpretation of nature consists in the examination of the history of nature, and therefrom deducing definitions of natural phenomena on certain fixed axioms, so Scriptural interpretation proceeds by the examination of Scripture, and inferring the intention of its authors as a legitimate conclusion from its fundamental principles. By working in this manner everyone will always advance without danger of error—that is, if they admit no principles for interpreting Scripture, and discussing its contents save such as they find in Scripture itself—and will be able with equal security to discuss what surpasses our understanding, and what is known by the natural light of reason.

In order to make clear that such a method is not only correct, but is also the only one advisable, and that it agrees with that employed in interpreting nature, I must remark that Scripture very often treats of matters which cannot be deduced from principles known to reason: for it is chiefly made up of narratives and revelation: the narratives generally contain miracles—that is, as we have shown in the last chapter, relations of extraordinary natural occurrences adapted to the opinions and judgment of the historians who recorded them: the revelations also were adapted to the opinions of the prophets, as we showed in Chap. ii., and in themselves surpassed human comprehension. Therefore the knowledge of all these—that is, of nearly the whole contents of Scripture, must be sought from Scripture alone, even as the knowledge of nature is sought from nature. As for the moral doctrines which are also contained in the Bible, they may be demonstrated from received axioms, but we cannot prove in the same manner that Scripture intended to teach them, this can only be learned from Scripture itself.

If we would bear unprejudiced witness to the Divine origin of Scripture, we must prove solely on its own authority that it teaches true moral doctrines, for by such means alone can its Divine origin be demonstrated: we have shown that the certitude of the prophets depended chiefly on their having minds turned towards what is just and good, therefore we ought to have proof of their possessing this quality before we repose faith in them. From miracles God's divinity cannot be proved, as I have already shown, and need not now repeat, for miracles could be wrought by false prophets. Wherefore the Divine origin of Scripture must consist solely in its teaching true virtue. But we must come to our conclusion simply on Scriptural grounds, for if we were unable to do so we could not, unless strongly prejudiced accept the Bible and bear witness to its Divine origin.

Our knowledge of Scripture must then be looked for in Scripture only.

Lastly, Scripture does not give us definition of things any more than nature does: therefore, such definitions must be sought in the latter case from the diverse workings of nature; in the former case, from the various narratives about the given subject which occur in the Bible.

The universal rule, then, in interpreting Scripture is to accept nothing as an authoritative Scriptural statement which we do not perceive very clearly when we examine it in the light of its history. What I mean by its history, and what should be the chief points elucidated, I will now explain.

The history of a Scriptural statement comprises—

I.   The nature and properties of the language in which the books of the Bible were written, and in which their authors were, accustomed to speak. We shall thus be able to investigate every expression by comparison with common conversational usages.

Now all the writers both of the Old Testament and the New were Hebrews: therefore, a knowledge of the Hebrew language is before all things necessary, not only for the comprehension of the Old Testament, which was written in that tongue, but also of the New: for although the latter was published in other languages, yet its characteristics are Hebrew.

II.   An analysis of each book and arrangement of its contents under heads; so that we may have at hand the various texts which treat of a given subject. Lastly, a note of all the passages which are ambiguous or obscure, or which seem mutually contradictory.

I call passages clear or obscure according as their meaning is inferred easily or with difficulty in relation to the context, not according as their truth is perceived easily or the reverse by reason. We are at work not on the truth of passages, but solely on their meaning. We must take especial care, when we are in search of the meaning of a text, not to be led away by our reason in so far as it is founded on principles of natural knowledge (to say nothing of prejudices): in order not to confound the meaning of a passage with its truth, we must examine it solely by means of the signification of the words, or by a reason acknowledging no foundation but Scripture.

I will illustrate my meaning by an example. The words of Moses, "God is a fire" and "God is jealous," are perfectly clear so long as we regard merely the signification of the words, and I therefore reckon them

among the clear passages, though in relation to reason and truth they are most obscure: still, although the literal meaning is repugnant to the natural light of reason, nevertheless, if it cannot be clearly overruled on grounds and principles derived from its Scriptural "history," it, that is, the literal meaning, must be the one retained: and contrariwise if these passages literally interpreted are found to clash with principles derived from Scripture, though such literal interpretation were in absolute harmony with reason, they must be interpreted in a different manner, i.e. metaphorically.

If we would know whether Moses believed God to be a fire or not, we must on no account decide the question on grounds of the reasonableness or the reverse of such an opinion, but must judge solely by the other opinions of Moses which are on record.

In the present instance, as Moses says in several other passages that God has no likeness to any visible thing, whether in heaven or in earth, or in the water, either all such passages must be taken metaphorically, or else the one before us must be so explained. However, as we should depart as little as possible from the literal sense, we must first ask whether this text, God is a fire, admits of any but the literal meaning—that is, whether the word fire ever means anything besides ordinary natural fire. If no such second meaning can be found, the text must be taken literally, however repugnant to reason it may be: and all the other passages, though in complete accordance with reason, must be brought into harmony with it. If the verbal expressions would not admit of being thus harmonized, we should have to set them down as irreconcilable, and suspend our judgment concerning them. However, as we find the name fire applied to anger and jealousy (see Job xxxi:12) we can thus easily reconcile the words

BARUCH SPINOZA

of Moses, and legitimately conclude that the two propositions God is a fire, and God is jealous, are in meaning identical.

Further, as Moses clearly teaches that God is jealous, and no-where states that God is without passions or emotions, we must evidently infer that Moses held this doctrine himself, or at any rate, that he wished to teach it, nor must we refrain because such a belief seems contrary to reason: for as we have shown, we cannot wrest the meaning of texts to suit the dictates of our reason, or our preconceived opinions. The whole knowledge of the Bible must be sought solely from itself.

III.   Lastly, such a history should relate the environment of all the prophetic books extant; that is, the life, the conduct, and the studies of the author of each book, who he was, what was the occasion, and the epoch of his writing, whom did he write for, and in what language. Further, it should inquire into the fate of each book: how it was first received, into whose hands it fell, how many different versions there were of it, by whose advice was it received into the Bible, and, lastly, how all the books now universally accepted as sacred, were united into a single whole.

All such information should, as I have said, be contained in the "history" of Scripture. For, in order to know what statements are set forth as laws, and what as moral precepts, it is impor-tant to be acquainted with the life, the conduct, and the pur-suits of their author: moreover, it becomes easier to explain a man's writings in proportion as we have more intimate knowl-edge of his genius and temperament.

Further, that we may not confound precepts which are eternal with those which served only a temporary purpose, or were only meant for a few, we should know what was the occasion, the time, the age, in which each book was written, and to what nation it was addressed.Lastly, we should have knowledge on the other points I have mentioned, in order to be sure, in addi-tion to the authenticity of the work, that it has not been tam-pered with by sacrilegious hands, or whether errors can have crept in, and, if so, whether they have been corrected by men sufficiently skilled and worthy of credence. All these things should be known, that we may not be led away by blind impulse to accept whatever is thrust on our notice, instead of only that which is sure and indisputable.

Now when we are in possession of this history of Scripture, and have finally decided that we assert nothing as prophetic doctrine which does not directly follow from such history, or which is not clearly deducible from it, then, I say, it will be time to gird ourselves for the task of investigating the mind of the prophets and of the Holy Spirit. But in this further arguing, also, we shall require a method very like that employed in interpreting nature from her history. As in the examination of natural phenomena we try first to investigate what is most universal and common to all nature—such, for instance, as motion and rest, and their laws and rules, which nature always observes, and through which she continually works—and then we proceed to what is less universal; so, too, in the history of Scripture, we seek first for that which is most universal, and serves for the basis and foundation of all Scripture, a doctrine, in fact, that is commended by all the prophets as eternal and most profitable to all men. For example, that God is one, and that He is omnipotent, that He alone should be worshipped, that He has a care for all men, and that He especially loves those who adore Him and love their neighbour as themselves, &c. These and similar doctrines, I repeat, Scripture everywhere so clearly and expressly teaches, that no one was ever in doubt of its meaning concerning them.

The nature of God, His manner of regarding and providing for things, and similar doctrines, Scripture nowhere teaches professedly, and as eternal doctrine; on the contrary, we have shown that the prophets themselves did not agree on the subject; therefore, we must not lay down any doctrine as Scriptural on such subjects, though it may appear perfectly clear on rational grounds.

From a proper knowledge of this universal doctrine of Scripture, we must then proceed to other doctrines less universal, but which, nevertheless, have regard to the general conduct of life, and flow from the universal doctrine like rivulets from a source; such are all particular external manifestations of true virtue, which need a given occasion for their exercise; whatever is obscure or ambiguous on such points in Scripture must be explained and defined by its universal doctrine; with regard to contradictory instances, we must observe the occasion and the time in which they were written. For instance, when Christ says, "Blessed are they that mourn, for they shall be comforted" we do not know, from the actual passage, what sort of mourners are meant; as, however, Christ afterwards teaches that we should have care for nothing, save only for the kingdom of God and His righteousness, which is commended as the highest good (see Matt. vi;33), it follows that by mourners He only meant those who mourn for the kingdom of God and righteousness neglected by man: for this would be the only cause of mourning to those who love nothing but the Divine kingdom and justice, and who evidently despise the gifts of fortune. So, too, when Christ says: "But if a man strike you on the right cheek, turn to him the left also," and the words which follow.

If He had given such a command, as a lawgiver, to judges, He would thereby have abrogated the law of Moses, but this He expressly says He did not do (Matt. v:17). Wherefore we must consider who was the speaker, what was the occasion, and to whom were the words addressed. Now Christ said that He did not ordain laws as a legislator, but inculcated precepts as a teacher: inasmuch as He did not aim at correcting outward actions so much as the frame of mind. Further, these words were spoken to men who were oppressed, who lived in a corrupt commonwealth on the brink of ruin, where justice was utterly neglected. The very doctrine inculcated here by Christ just before the destruction of the city was also taught by Jeremiah before the first destruction of Jerusalem, that is, in similar circumstances, as we see from Lamentations iii:25-30.

Now as such teaching was only set forth by the prophets in times of oppression, and was even then never laid down as a law; and as, on the other hand, Moses (who did not write in times of oppression, but—mark this—strove to found a well-ordered commonwealth), while condemning envy and hatred of one's neighbour, yet ordained that an eye should be given for an eye, it follows most clearly from these purely Scriptural grounds that this precept of Christ and Jeremiah concerning submission to injuries was only valid in places where justice is neglected, and in a time of oppression, but does not hold good in a well-ordered state.

In a well-ordered state where justice is administered every one is bound, if he would be accounted just, to demand penalties before the judge (see Lev:1), not for the sake of vengeance (Lev. xix:17, 18), but in order to defend justice and his country's laws, and to prevent the wicked rejoicing in their wickedness. All this is plainly in accordance with reason. I might cite many other examples in the same manner, but I think the foregoing are sufficient to explain my meaning and the utility of this method, and this is all my present purpose. Hitherto we have only shown how to investigate those passages of Scripture which treat of practical conduct, and which, therefore, are more easily examined, for on such subjects there was never really any controversy among the writers of the Bible.

The purely speculative passages cannot be so easily, traced to their real meaning: the way becomes narrower, for as the prophets differed in matters speculative among themselves, and the narratives are in great measure adapted to the prejudices of each age, we must not, on any, account infer the intention of one prophet from clearer passages in the writings of another; nor must we so explain his meaning, unless it is perfectly plain that the two prophets were at one in the matter.

How we are to arrive at the intention of the prophets in such cases I will briefly explain. Here, too, we must begin from the most universal proposition, inquiring first from the most clear Scriptural statements what is the nature of prophecy or revelation, and wherein does it consist; then we must proceed to miracles, and so on to whatever is most general till we come to the opinions of a particular prophet, and, at last, to the meaning of a particular revelation, prophecy, history, or miracle. We have already pointed out that great caution is necessary not to confound the mind of a prophet or historian with the mind of the Holy Spirit and the truth of the matter; therefore I need not dwell further on the subject. I would, however, here remark concerning the meaning of revelation, that the present method only teaches us what the prophets really saw or heard, not what they desired to signify or represent by symbols. The latter may be guessed at but cannot be inferred with certainty from Scriptural premises.

We have thus shown the plan for interpreting Scripture, and have, at the same time, demonstrated that it is the one and surest way of investigating its true meaning. I am willing indeed to admit that those persons (if any such there be) would be more absolutely certainly right, who have received either a trustworthy tradition or an assurance from the prophets themselves, such as is claimed by the Pharisees; or who have a pontiff gifted with infallibility in the interpretation of Scripture, such as the Roman Catholics boast. But as we can never be perfectly sure, either of such a tradition or of the authority of the pontiff, we cannot found any certain conclusion on either: the one is denied by the oldest sect of Christians, the other by the oldest sect of Jews. Indeed, if we consider the series of years (to mention no other point) accepted by the Pharisees from their Rabbis, during which time they say they have handed down the tradition from Moses, we shall find that it is not correct, as I show elsewhere. Therefore such a tradition should be received with extreme suspicion; and although, according to our method, we are bound to consider as uncorrupted the tradition of the Jews, namely, the meaning of the Hebrew words which we received from them, we may accept the latter while retaining our doubts about the former.

No one has ever been able to change the meaning of a word in ordinary use, though many have changed the meaning of a particular sentence. Such a proceeding would be most difficult; for whoever attempted to change the meaning of a word, would be compelled, at the same time, to explain all the authors who employed it, each according to his temperament and intention, or else, with consummate cunning, to falsify them.

Further, the masses and the learned alike preserve language, but it is only the learned who preserve the meaning of particular sentences and books: thus, we may easily imagine that the learned having a very rare book in their power, might change or corrupt the meaning of a sentence in it, but they could not alter the signification of the words; moreover, if anyone wanted to change the meaning of a common word he would not be able to keep up the change among posterity, or in common parlance or writing.

For these and such-like reasons we may readily conclude that it would never enter into the mind of anyone to corrupt a language, though the intention of a writer may often have been falsified by changing his phrases or interpreting them amiss. As then our method (based on the principle that the knowledge of Scripture must be sought from itself alone) is the sole true one, we must evidently renounce any knowledge which it cannot furnish for the complete understanding of Scripture. I will now point out its difficulties and shortcomings, which prevent our gaining a complete and assured knowledge of the Sacred Text.

Its first great difficulty consists in its requiring a thorough knowledge of the Hebrew language. Where is such knowledge to be obtained? The men of old who employed the Hebrew tongue have left none of the principles and bases of their language to posterity; we have from them absolutely nothing in the way of dictionary, grammar, or rhetoric.

Now the Hebrew nation has lost all its grace and beauty (as one would expect after the defeats and persecutions it has gone through), and has only retained certain fragments of its language and of a few books. Nearly all the names of fruits, birds, and fishes, and many other words have perished in the wear and tear of time. Further, the meaning of many nouns and verbs which occur in the Bible are either utterly lost, or are subjects of dispute. And not only are these gone, but we are lacking in a knowledge of Hebrew phraseology. The devouring tooth of time has destroyed turns of expression peculiar to the Hebrews, so that we know them no more.

Therefore we cannot investigate as we would all the meanings of a sentence by the uses of the language; and there are many phrases of which the meaning is most obscure or altogether inexplicable, though the component words are perfectly plain.

To this impossibility of tracing the history of the Hebrew language must be added its particular nature and composition: these give rise to so many ambiguities that it is impossible to find a method which would enable us to gain a certain knowledge of all the statements in Scripture,[2] In addition to the sources of ambiguities common to all languages, there are many peculiar to Hebrew. These, I think, it worth while to mention.

Firstly, an ambiguity often arises in the Bible from our mistaking one letter for another similar one. The Hebrews divide the letters of the alphabet into five classes, according to the five organs of the month employed in pronouncing them, namely, the lips, the tongue, the teeth, the palate, and the throat. For instance, Alpha, Ghet, Hgain, He, are called gutturals, and are barely distinguishable, by any sign that we know, one from the other. El, which signifies to, is often taken for hgal, which signifies above, and vice versa. Hence sentences are often rendered rather ambiguous or meaningless.

A second difficulty arises from the multiplied meaning of conjunctions and adverbs. For instance, vau serves promiscuously for a particle of union or of separation, meaning, and, but, because, however, then: ki, has seven or eight meanings, namely, wherefore, although, if, when, inasmuch as, because, a burning, &c., and so on with almost all particles.

The third very fertile source of doubt is the fact that Hebrew verbs in the indicative mood lack the present, the past imperfect, the pluperfect, the future perfect, and other tenses most frequently employed in other languages; in the imperative and infinitive moods they are wanting in all except the present, and a subjunctive mood does not exist. Now, although all these defects in moods and tenses may be supplied by certain fundamental rules of the language with ease and even elegance, the ancient writers evidently neglected such rules altogether, and employed indifferently future for present and past, and vice versa past for future, and also indicative for imperative and subjunctive, with the result of considerable confusion.

---

2   See Endnote 7.

Besides these sources of ambiguity there are two others, one very important. Firstly, there are in Hebrew no vowels; secondly, the sentences are not separated by any marks elucidating the meaning or separating the clauses. Though the want of these two has generally been supplied by points and accents, such substitutes cannot be accepted by us, inasmuch as they were invented and designed by men of an after age whose authority should carry no weight. The ancients wrote without points (that is, without vowels and accents), as is abundantly testified; their descendants added what was lacking, according to their own ideas of Scriptural interpretation; wherefore the existing accents and points are simply current interpretations, and are no more authoritative than any other commentaries.

Those who are ignorant of this fact cannot justify the author of the Epistle to the Hebrews for interpreting (chap. xi;21) Genesis (xlvii:31) very differently from the version given in our Hebrew text as at present pointed, as though the Apostle had been obliged to learn the meaning of Scripture from those who added the points. In my opinion the latter are clearly wrong. In order that everyone may judge for himself, and also see how the discrepancy arose simply from the want of vowels, I will give both interpretations. Those who pointed our version read, "And Israel bent himself over, or (changing Hqain into Aleph, a similar letter) towards, the head of the bed." The author of the Epistle reads, "And Israel bent himself over the head of his staff," substituting mate for mita, from which it only differs in respect of vowels. Now as in this narrative it is Jacob's age only that is in question, and not his illness, which is not touched on till the next chapter, it seems more likely that the historian intended to say that Jacob bent over the head of his staff (a thing commonly used by men of advanced age for their support) than that he bowed himself at the head of his bed, especially as for the former reading no substitution of letters is required. In this example I have desired not only to reconcile the passage in the Epistle with the passage in Genesis, but also and chiefly to illustrate how little trust should be placed in the points and accents which are found in our present Bible, and so to prove that he who would be without bias in interpreting Scripture should hesitate about accepting them, and inquire afresh for himself. Such being the nature and structure of the Hebrew language, one may easily understand that many difficulties are likely to arise, and that no possible method could solve all of them. It is useless to hope for a way out of our difficulties in the comparison of various parallel passages (we have shown that the only method of discovering the true sense of a passage out of many alternative ones is to see what are the usages of the language), for this comparison of parallel passages can only accidentally throw light on a difficult point, seeing that the prophets never wrote with the express object of explaining their own phrases or those of other people, and also because we cannot infer the meaning of one prophet or apostle by the meaning of another, unless on a purely practical question, not when the matter is speculative, or if a miracle, or history is being narrated. I might illustrate my point with instances, for there are many inexplicable phrases in Scripture, but I would rather pass on to consider the difficulties and imperfections of the method under discussion.

A further difficulty attends the method, from the fact that it requires the history of all that has happened to every book in the Bible; such a history we are often quite unable to furnish. Of the authors, or (if the expression be preferred), the writers of many of the books, we are either in complete ignorance, or at any rate in doubt, as I will point out at length. Further, we do not know either the occasions or the epochs when these books of unknown authorship were written; we cannot say into what hands they fell, nor how the numerous varying versions originated; nor, lastly, whether there were not other versions, now lost. I have briefly shown that such knowledge is necessary, but I passed over certain considerations which I will now draw attention to.

If we read a book which contains incredible or impossible narratives, or is written in a very obscure style, and if we know nothing of its author, nor of the time or occasion of its being written, we shall vainly endeavour to gain any certain knowledge of its true meaning. For being in ignorance on these points we cannot possibly know the aim or intended aim of the author; if we are fully informed, we so order our thoughts as not to be in any way prejudiced either in ascribing to the author or him for whom the author wrote either more or less than his meaning, and we only take into consideration what the author may have had in his mind, or what the time and occasion demanded. I think this must be tolerably evident to all.

It often happens that in different books we read histories in themselves similar, but which we judge very differently, according to the opinions we have formed of the authors. I remember once to have read in some book that a man named Orlando Furioso used to drive a kind of winged monster through the air, fly over any countries he liked, kill unaided vast numbers of men and giants, and such like fancies, which from the point of view of reason are obviously absurd. A very similar story I read in Ovid of Perseus, and also in the books of Judges and Kings of Samson, who alone and unarmed killed thousands of men, and of Elijah, who flew through the air, said at last went up to heaven in a chariot of fire, with horses of fire. All these stories are obviously alike, but we judge them very differently. The first only sought to amuse, the second had a political object, the third a religious object.We gather this simply from the opinions we had previously formed of the authors. Thus it is evidently necessary to know something of the authors of writings which are obscure or unintelligible, if we would interpret their meaning; and for the same reason, in order to choose the proper reading from among a great variety, we ought to have information as to the versions in which the differences are found, and as to the possibility of other readings having been discovered by persons of greater authority.

A further difficulty attends this method in the case of some of the books of Scripture, namely, that they are no longer extant in their original language. The Gospel according to Matthew, and certainly the Epistle to the Hebrews, were written, it is thought, in Hebrew, though they no longer exist in that form. Aben Ezra affirms in his commentaries that the book of Job was translated into Hebrew out of another language, and that its obscurity arises from this fact. I say nothing of the apocryphal books, for their authority stands on very inferior ground.

The foregoing difficulties in this method of interpreting Scripture from its own history, I conceive to be so great that I do not hesitate to say that the true meaning of Scripture is in many places inexplicable, or at best mere subject for guesswork; but I must again point out, on the other hand, that such difficulties only arise when we endeavour to follow the meaning of a prophet in matters which cannot be perceived, but only imagined, not in things, whereof the understanding can give a clear idea, and which are conceivable through themselves:,[3] matters which by their nature are easily perceived cannot be expressed so obscurely as to be unintelligible; as the proverb says, "a word is enough to the wise." Euclid, who only wrote of matters very simple and easily understood, can easily be comprehended by anyone in any language; we can follow his intention perfectly, and be certain of his true meaning, without having a thorough knowledge of the language in which he wrote; in fact, a quite rudimentary acquaintance is sufficient. We need make no researches concerning the life, the pursuits, or the habits of the author; nor need we inquire in what language, nor when he wrote, nor the vicissitudes of his book, nor its various readings, nor how, nor by whose advice it has been received.

What we here say of Euclid might equally be said of any book which treats of things by their nature perceptible: thus we conclude that we can easily follow the intention of Scripture in moral questions, from the history we possess of it, and we can be sure of its true meaning.

The precepts of true piety are expressed in very ordinary language, and are equally simple and easily understood. Further, as true salvation and blessedness consist in a true assent of the soul—and we truly assent only to what we clearly understand—it is most plain that we can follow with certainty the intention of Scripture in matters relating to salvation and necessary to blessedness; therefore, we need not be much troubled about what remains: such matters, inasmuch as we generally cannot grasp them with our reason and understanding, are more curious than profitable.

3   See Endnote 8.

I think I have now set forth the true method of Scriptural interpretation, and have sufficiently explained my own opinion thereon. Besides, I do not doubt that everyone will see that such a method only requires the aid of natural reason. The nature and efficacy of the natural reason consists in deducing and proving the unknown from the known, or in carrying premises to their legitimate conclusions; and these are the very processes which our method desiderates. Though we must admit that it does not suffice to explain everything in the Bible, such imperfection does not spring from its own nature, but from the fact that the path which it teaches us, as the true one, has never been tended or trodden by men, and has thus, by the lapse of time, become very difficult, and almost impassable, as, indeed, I have shown in the difficulties I draw attention to.

There only remains to examine the opinions of those who differ from me. The first which comes under our notice is, that the light of nature has no power to interpret Scripture, but that a supernatural faculty is required for the task. What is meant by this supernatural faculty I will leave to its propounders to explain. Personally, I can only suppose that they have adopted a very obscure way of stating their complete uncertainty about the true meaning of Scripture. If we look at their interpretations, they contain nothing supernatural, at least nothing but the merest conjectures.

Let them be placed side by side with the interpretations of those who frankly confess that they have no faculty beyond their natural ones; we shall see that the two are just alike—both human, both long pondered over, both laboriously invented. To say that the natural reason is insufficient for such results is plainly untrue, firstly, for the reasons above stated, namely, that the difficulty of interpreting Scripture arises from no defect in human reason, but simply from the carelessness (not to say malice) of men who neglected the history of the Bible while there were still materials for inquiry; secondly, from the fact (admitted, I think, by all) that the supernatural faculty is a Divine gift granted only to the faithful. But the prophets and apostles did not preach to the faithful only, but chiefly to the unfaithful and wicked. Such persons, therefore, were able to understand the intention of the prophets and apostles, otherwise the prophets and apostles would have seemed to be preaching to little boys and infants, not to men endowed with reason. Moses, too, would have given his laws in vain, if they could only be comprehended by the faithful, who need no law. Indeed, those who demand supernatural faculties for comprehending the meaning of the prophets and apostles seem truly lacking in natural faculties, so that we should hardly suppose such persons the possessors of a Divine supernatural gift.

The opinion of Maimonides was widely different. He asserted that each passage in Scripture admits of various, nay, contrary, meanings; but that we could never be certain of any particular one till we knew that the passage, as we interpreted it, contained nothing contrary or repugnant to reason. If the literal meaning clashes with reason, though the passage seems in itself perfectly clear, it must be interpreted in some metaphorical sense. This doctrine he lays down very plainly in chap. xxv. part ii. of his book, "More Nebuchim," for he says: "Know that we shrink not from affirming that the world hath existed from eternity, because of what Scripture saith concerning the world's creation. For the texts which teach that the world was created are not more in number than those which teach that God hath a body; neither are the approaches in this matter of the world's creation closed, or even made hard to us: so that we should not be able to explain what is written, as we did when we showed that God hath no body, nay, peradventure, we could explain and make fast the doctrine of the world's eternity more easily than we did away with the doctrines that God hath a beatified body. Yet two things hinder me from doing as I have said, and believing that the world is eternal. As it hath been clearly shown that God hath not a body, we must perforce explain all those passages whereof the literal sense agreeth not with the demonstration, for sure it is that they can be so explained. But the eternity of the world hath not been so demonstrated, therefore it is not necessary to do violence to Scripture in support of some common opinion, whereof we might, at the bidding of reason, embrace the contrary."

Such are the words of Maimonides, and they are evidently sufficient to establish our point: for if he had been convinced by reason that the world is eternal, he would not have hesitated to twist and explain away the words of Scripture till he made them appear to teach this doctrine. He would have felt quite sure that Scripture, though everywhere plainly denying the eternity of the world, really intends to teach it. So that, however clear the meaning of Scripture may be, he would not feel certain of having grasped it, so long as he remained doubtful of the truth of what, was written. For we are in doubt whether a thing is in conformity with reason, or contrary thereto, so long as we are uncertain of its truth, and, consequently, we cannot be sure whether the literal meaning of a passage be true or false.

If such a theory as this were sound, I would certainly grant that some faculty beyond the natural reason is required for interpreting Scripture. For nearly all things that we find in Scripture cannot be inferred from known principles of the natural reason, and, therefore, we should be unable to come to any conclusion about their truth, or about the real meaning and intention of Scripture, but should stand in need of some further assistance.

Further, the truth of this theory would involve that the masses, having generally no comprehension of, nor leisure for, detailed proofs, would be reduced to receiving all their knowledge of Scripture on the authority and testimony of philosophers, and, consequently, would be compelled to suppose that the interpretations given by philosophers were infallible.

Truly this would be a new form of ecclesiastical authority, and a new sort of priests or pontiffs, more likely to excite men's ridicule than their veneration. Certainly our method demands a knowledge of Hebrew for which the masses have no leisure; but no such objection as the foregoing can be brought against us. For the ordinary Jews or Gentiles, to whom the prophets and apostles preached and wrote, understood the language, and, consequently, the intention of the prophet or apostle addressing them; but they did not grasp the intrinsic reason of what was preached, which, according to Maimonides, would be necessary for an understanding of it.

There is nothing, then, in our method which renders it necessary that the masses should follow the testimony of commentators, for I point to a set of unlearned people who understood the language of the prophets and apostles; whereas Maimonides could not point to any such who could arrive at the prophetic or apostolic meaning through their knowledge of the causes of things.

As to the multitude of our own time, we have shown that whatsoever is necessary to salvation, though its reasons may be unknown, can easily be understood in any language, because it is thoroughly ordinary and usual; it is in such understanding as this that the masses acquiesce, not in the testimony of commentators; with regard to other questions, the ignorant and the learned fare alike.

But let us return to the opinion of Maimonides, and examine it more closely. In the first place, he supposes that the prophets were in entire agreement one with another, and that they were consummate philosophers and theologians; for he would have them to have based their conclusions on the absolute truth. Further, he supposes that the sense of Scripture cannot be made plain from Scripture itself, for the truth of things is not made plain therein (in that it does not prove any thing, nor teach the matters of which it speaks through their definitions and first causes), therefore, according to Maimonides, the true sense of Scripture cannot be made plain from itself, and must not be there sought.

The falsity of such a doctrine is shown in this very chapter, for we have shown both by reason and examples that the meaning of Scripture is only made plain through Scripture itself, and even in questions deducible from ordinary knowledge should be looked for from no other source.

Lastly, such a theory supposes that we may explain the words of Scripture according to our preconceived opinions, twisting them about, and reversing or completely changing the literal sense, however plain it may be. Such licence is utterly opposed to the teaching of this and the preceding chapters, and, moreover, will be evident to everyone as rash and excessive.

But if we grant all this licence, what can it effect after all? Absolutely nothing. Those things which cannot be demonstrated, and which make up the greater part of Scripture, cannot be examined by reason, and cannot therefore be explained or interpreted by this rule; whereas, on the contrary, by following our own method, we can explain many questions of this nature, and discuss them on a sure basis, as we have already shown, by reason and example. Those matters which are by their nature comprehensible we can easily explain, as has been pointed out, simply by means of the context.

Therefore, the method of Maimonides is clearly useless: to which we may add, that it does away with all the certainty which the masses acquire by candid reading, or which is gained by any other persons in any other way. In conclusion, then, we dismiss Maimonides' theory as harmful, useless, and absurd.

As to the tradition of the Pharisees, we have already shown that it is not consistent, while the authority of the popes of Rome stands in need of more credible evidence; the latter, indeed, I reject simply on this ground, for if the popes could point out to us the meaning of Scripture as surely as did the high priests of the Jews, I should not be deterred by the fact that there have been heretic and impious Roman pontiffs; for among the Hebrew high-priests of old there were also heretics and impious men who gained the high-priesthood by improper means, but who, nevertheless, had Scriptural sanction for their supreme power of interpreting the law. (See Deut. xvii:11, 12, and xxxiii:10, also Malachi ii:8.)

However, as the popes can show no such sanction, their authority remains open to very grave doubt, nor should anyone be deceived by the example of the Jewish high-priests and think that the Catholic religion also stands in need of a pontiff; he should bear in mind that the laws of Moses being also the ordinary laws of the country, necessarily required some public authority to insure their observance; for, if everyone were free to interpret the laws of his country as he pleased, no state could stand, but would for that very reason be dissolved at once, and public rights would become private rights.

With religion the case is widely different. Inasmuch as it consists not so much in outward actions as in simplicity and truth of character, it stands outside the sphere of law and public authority. Simplicity and truth of character are not produced by the constraint of laws, nor by the authority of the state, no one the whole world over can be forced or legislated into a state of blessedness; the means required for such a consummation are faithful and brotherly admonition, sound education, and, above all, free use of the individual judgment.

Therefore, as the supreme right of free thinking, even on religion, is in every man's power, and as it is inconceivable that such power could be alienated, it is also in every man's power to wield the supreme right and authority of free judgment in this behalf, and to explain and interpret religion for himself. The only reason for vesting the supreme authority in the interpretation of law, and judgment on public affairs in the hands of the magistrates, is that it concerns questions of public right. Similarly the supreme authority in explaining religion, and in passing judgment thereon, is lodged with the individual because it concerns questions of individual right. So far, then, from the authority of the Hebrew high-priests telling in confirmation of the authority of the Roman pontiffs to interpret religion, it would rather tend to establish individual freedom of judgment. Thus in this way also, we have shown that our method of interpreting Scripture is the best. For as the highest power of Scriptural interpretation belongs to every man, the rule for such interpretation should be nothing but the natural light of reason which is common to all—not any supernatural light nor any external authority; moreover, such a rule ought not to be so difficult that it can only be applied by very skilful philosophers, but should be adapted to the natural and ordinary faculties and capacity of mankind. And such I have shown our method to be, for such difficulties as it has arise from men's carelessness, and are no part of its nature.

CHAPTER VIII

Of the Authorship of the Pentateuch and the Other Historical Books of the Old Testament

IN the former chapter we treated of the foundations and principles of Scriptural knowledge, and showed that it consists solely in a trustworthy history of the sacred writings; such a history, in spite of its indispensability, the ancients neglected, or at any rate, whatever they may have written or handed down has perished in the lapse of time, consequently the groundwork for such an investigation is to a great extent, cut from under us. This might be put up with if succeeding generations had confined themselves within the limits of truth, and had handed down conscientiously what few particulars they had received or discovered without any additions from their own brains: as it is, the history of the Bible is not so much imperfect as untrustworthy: the foundations are not only too scanty for building upon, but are also unsound. It is part of my purpose to remedy these defects, and to remove common theological prejudices. But I fear that I am attempting my task too late, for men have arrived at the pitch of not suffering contradiction, but defending obstinately whatever they have adopted under the name of religion. So widely have these prejudices taken possession of men's minds, that very few, comparatively speaking, will listen to reason. However, I will make the attempt, and spare no efforts, for there is no positive reason for despairing of success.

In order to treat the subject methodically, I will begin with the received opinions concerning the true authors of the sacred

books, and in the first place, speak of the author of the Pentateuch, who is almost universally supposed to have been Moses.
The Pharisees are so firmly convinced of his identity, that they
account as a heretic anyone who differs from them on the subject. Wherefore, Aben Ezra, a man of enlightened intelligence,
and no small learning, who was the first, so far as I know, to
treat of this opinion, dared not express his meaning openly,
but confined himself to dark hints which I shall not scruple to
elucidate, thus throwing, full light on the subject.

The words of Aben Ezra which occur in his commentary on
Deuteronomy are as follows: "Beyond Jordan, &c . . . If so be
that thou understandest the mystery of the twelve . . . moreover Moses wrote the law . . . The Canaanite was then in the
land . . . . it shall be revealed on the mount of God . . . . then
also behold his bed, his iron bed, then shalt thou know the
truth." In these few words he hints, and also shows that it was
not Moses who wrote the Pentateuch, but someone who lived
long after him, and further, that the book which Moses wrote
was something different from any now extant.

To prove this, I say, he draws attention to the facts:

I.   That the preface to Deuteronomy could not have been
written by Moses, inasmuch as he ad never crossed the Jordan.

II.   That the whole book of Moses was written at full
length on the circumference of a single altar (Deut. xxvii, and
Josh. viii:37), which altar, according to the Rabbis, consisted
of only twelve stones: therefore the book of Moses must have
been of far less extent than the Pentateuch. This is what our
author means, I think, by the mystery of the twelve, unless
he is referring to the twelve curses contained in the chapter
of Deuteronomy above cited, which he thought could not have
been contained in the law, because Moses bade the Levites
read them after the recital of the law, and so bind the people to
its observance. Or again, he may have had in his mind the last
chapter of Deuteronomy which treats of the death of Moses,
and which contains twelve verses. But there is no need to dwell
further on these and similar conjectures.

III.   That in Deut. xxxi:9, the expression occurs, "and Moses wrote the law:" words that cannot be ascribed to Moses, but must be those of some other writer narrating the deeds and writings of Moses.

IV.   That in Genesis xii:6, the historian, after narrating that Abraham journeyed through the and of Canaan, adds, "and the Canaanite was then in the land," thus clearly excluding the time at which he wrote. So that this passage must have been written after the death of Moses, when the Canaanites had been driven out, and no longer possessed the land.

Aben Ezra, in his commentary on the passage, alludes to the difficulty as follows:—"And the Canaanite was then in the land: it appears that Canaan, the grandson of Noah, took from another the land which bears his name; if this be not the true meaning, there lurks some mystery in the passage, and let him who understands it keep silence." That is, if Canaan invaded those regions, the sense will be, the Canaanite was then in the land, in contradistinction to the time when it had been held by another: but if, as follows from Gen. chap. x. Canaan was the first to inhabit the land, the text must mean to exclude the time present, that is the time at which it was written; therefore it cannot be the work of Moses, in whose time the Canaanites still possessed those territories: this is the mystery concerning which silence is recommended.

V.   That in Genesis xxii:14 Mount Moriah is called the mount of God,[4] a name which it did not acquire till after the building of the Temple; the choice of the mountain was not made in the time of Moses, for Moses does not point out any spot as chosen by God; on the contrary, he foretells that God will at some future time choose a spot to which this name will be given.

VI.   Lastly, that in Deut. chap. iii., in the passage relating to Og, king of Bashan, these words are inserted: "For only Og king of Bashan remained of the remnant of giants: behold, his bedstead was a bedstead of iron: is it not in Rabbath of the children of Ammon? nine cubits was the length thereof, and

---

4   See Endnote 9.

four cubits the breadth of it, after the cubit of a man." This parenthesis most plainly shows that its writer lived long after Moses; for this mode of speaking is only employed by one treating of things long past, and pointing to relics for the sake of gaining credence: moreover, this bed was almost certainly first discovered by David, who conquered the city of Rabbath (2 Sam. xii:30.) Again, the historian a little further on inserts after the words of Moses, "Jair, the son of Manasseh, took all the country of Argob unto the coasts of Geshuri and Maachathi; and called them after his own name, Bashan-havoth-jair, unto this day." This passage, I say, is inserted to explain the words of Moses which precede it. "And the rest of Gilead, and all Bashan, being the kingdom of Og, gave I unto the half tribe of Manasseh; all the region of Argob, with all Bashan, which is called the land of the giants." The Hebrews in the time of the writer indisputably knew what territories belonged to the tribe of Judah, but did not know them under the name of the jurisdiction of Argob, or the land of the giants. Therefore the writer is compelled to explain what these places were which were anciently so styled, and at the same time to point out why they were at the time of his writing known by the name of Jair, who was of the tribe of Manasseh, not of Judah. We have thus made clear the meaning of Aben Ezra and also the passages of the Pentateuch which he cites in proof of his contention. However, Aben Ezra does not call attention to every instance, or even the chief ones; there remain many of greater importance, which may be cited. Namely,

I.   That the writer of the books in question not only speaks of Moses in the third person, but also bears witness to many details concerning him; for instance, "Moses talked with God;" "The Lord spoke with Moses face to face; " "Moses was the meekest of men" (Numb. xii:3); "Moses was wrath with the captains of the host; "Moses, the man of God, "Moses, the servant of the Lord, died;" "There was never a prophet in Israel like unto Moses," &c. On the other hand, in Deuteronomy, where the law which Moses had expounded to the people and written is set forth, Moses speaks and declares what he has done in the first person: "God spake with me " (Deut. ii:1,

17, &c.), "I prayed to the Lord," &c. Except at the end of the book, when the historian, after relating the words of Moses, begins again to speak in the third person, and to tell how Moses handed over the law which he had expounded to the people in writing, again admonishing them, and further, how Moses ended his life. All these details, the manner of narration, the testimony, and the context of the whole story lead to the plain conclusion that these books were written by another, and not by Moses in person.

II. We must also remark that the history relates not only the manner of Moses' death and burial, and the thirty days' mourning of the Hebrews, but further compares him with all the prophets who came after him, and states that he surpassed them all. "There was never a prophet in Israel like unto Moses, whom the Lord knew face to face." Such testimony cannot have been given of Moses by, himself, nor by any who immediately succeeded him, but it must come from someone who lived centuries afterwards, especially, as the historian speaks of past times. "There was never a prophet," &c. And of the place of burial, "No one knows it to this day."

III. We must note that some places are not styled by the names they bore during Moses' lifetime, but by others which they obtained subsequently. For instance, Abraham is said to have pursued his enemies even unto Dan, a name not bestowed on the city till long after the death of Joshua (Gen. xiv;14, Judges xviii;29).

IV. The narrative is prolonged after the death of Moses, for in Exodus xvi:34 we read that "the children of Israel did eat manna forty years until they came to a land inhabited, until they came unto the borders of the land of Canaan." In other words, until the time alluded to in Joshua vi:12.

So, too, in Genesis xxxvi:31 it is stated, "These are the kings that reigned in Edom before there reigned any king over the children of Israel." The historian, doubtless, here relates the kings of Idumaea before that territory was conquered by David[5] and garrisoned, as we read in 2 Sam. viii:14. From what has been said, it is thus clearer than the sun at noonday that the Pentateuch was not written by Moses, but by someone who lived long after Moses. Let us now turn our attention to the books which Moses actually did write, and which are cited in the Pentateuch; thus, also, shall we see that they were different from the Pentateuch. Firstly, it appears from Exodus xvii:14 that Moses, by the command of God, wrote an account of the war against Amalek. The book in which he did so is not named in the chapter just quoted, but in Numb. xxi:12 a book is referred to under the title of the wars of God, and doubtless this war against Amalek and the castrametations said in Numb. xxxiii:2 to have been written by Moses are therein described. We hear also in Exod. xxiv:4 of another book called the Book of the Covenant, which Moses read before the Israelites when they first made a covenant with God. But this book or this writing contained very little, namely, the laws or commandments of God which we find in Exodus xx:22 to the end of chap. xxiv., and this no one will deny who reads the aforesaid chapter rationally and impartially. It is there stated that as soon as Moses had learnt the feeling of the people on the subject of making a covenant with God, he immediately wrote down God's laws and utterances, and in the morning, after some ceremonies had been performed, read out the conditions of the covenant to an assembly of the whole people. When these had been gone through, and doubtless understood by all, the whole people gave their assent.

Now from the shortness of the time taken in its perusal and also from its nature as a compact, this document evidently contained nothing more than that which we have just described. Further, it is clear that Moses explained all the laws which he had received in the fortieth year after the exodus from Egypt; also that he bound over the people a second time to observe them, and that finally he committed them to writing (Deut. i:5; xxix:14; xxxi:9), in a book which contained these laws explained, and the new covenant, and this book was therefore called the book of the law of God: the same which was afterwards added to by Joshua when he set forth the fresh covenant

5   See Endnote 10.

with which he bound over the people and which he entered into with God (Josh. xxiv:25, 26).

Now, as we have extent no book containing this covenant of Moses and also the covenant of Joshua, we must perforce conclude that it has perished, unless, indeed, we adopt the wild conjecture of the Chaldean paraphrast Jonathan, and twist about the words of Scripture to our heart's content. This commentator, in the face of our present difficulty, preferred corrupting the sacred text to confessing his own ignorance. The passage in the book of Joshua which runs, "and Joshua wrote these words in the book of the law of God," he changes into "and Joshua wrote these words and kept them with the book of the law of God." What is to be done with persons who will only see what pleases them? What is such a proceeding if it is not denying Scripture, and inventing another Bible out of our own heads? We may therefore conclude that the book of the law of God which Moses wrote was not the Pentateuch, but something quite different, which the author of the Pentateuch duly inserted into his book. So much is abundantly plain both from what I have said and from what I am about to add. For in the passage of Deuteronomy above quoted, where it is related that Moses wrote the book of the law, the historian adds that he handed it over to the priests and bade them read it out at a stated time to the whole people. This shows that the work was of much less length than the Pentateuch, inasmuch as it could be read through at one sitting so as to be understood by all; further, we must not omit to notice that out of all the books which Moses wrote, this one book of the second covenant and the song (which latter he wrote afterwards so that all the people might learn it), was the only one which he caused to be religiously guarded and preserved. In the first covenant he had only bound over those who were present, but in the second covenant he bound over all their descendants also (Dent. xxix:14), and therefore ordered this covenant with future ages to be religiously preserved, together with the Song, which was especially addressed to posterity: as, then, we have no proof that Moses wrote any book save this of the covenant, and as he committed no other to the care of posterity; and, lastly, as there are many passages in the Pentateuch which Moses could not have written, it follows that the belief that Moses was the author of the Pentateuch is ungrounded and even irrational. Someone will perhaps ask whether Moses did not also write down other laws when they were first revealed to him—in other words, whether, during the course of forty years, he did not write down any of the laws which he promulgated, save only those few which I have stated to be contained in the book of the first covenant. To this I would answer, that although it seems reasonable to suppose that Moses wrote down the laws at the time when he wished to communicate them to the people, yet we are not warranted to take it as proved, for I have shown above that we must make no assertions in such matters which we do not gather from Scripture, or which do not flow as legitimate consequences from its fundamental principles. We must not accept whatever is reasonably probable. However even reason in this case would not force such a conclusion upon us: for it may be that the assembly of elders wrote down the decrees of Moses and communicated them to the people, and the historian collected them, and duly set them forth in his narrative of the life of Moses. So much for the five books of Moses: it is now time for us to turn to the other sacred writings.

The book of Joshua may be proved not to be an autograph by reasons similar to those we have just employed: for it must be some other than Joshua who testifies that the fame of Joshua was spread over the whole world; that he omitted nothing of what Moses had taught (Josh. vi:27; viii. last verse; xi:15); that he grew old and summoned an assembly of the whole people, and finally that he departed this life. Furthermore, events are related which took place after Joshua's death. For instance, that the Israelites worshipped God, after his death, so long as there were any old men alive who remembered him; and in chap. xvi:10, we read that "Ephraim and Manasseh did not drive out the Canaanites which dwelt in Gezer, but the Canaanite dwelt in the land of Ephraim unto this day, and was tributary to him." This is the same statement as that in Judges, chap. i., and the phrase "unto this day" shows that the writer was speaking of ancient times. With these texts we may compare the last verse of chap. xv., concerning the sons of Judah, and also the history of Caleb in the same chap. v:14. Further, the building of an altar beyond Jordan by the two tribes and a half, chap. xxii:10, sqq., seems to have taken place after the death of Joshua, for in the whole narrative his name is never mentioned, but the people alone held council as to waging war, sent out legates, waited for their return, and finally approved of their answer.

Lastly, from chap. x:14, it is clear that the book was written many generations after the death of Joshua, for it bears witness, there was never any, day like unto, that day, either before or after, that the Lord hearkened to the voice of a man," &c. If, therefore, Joshua wrote any book at all, it was that which is quoted in the work now before us, chap. x:13.

With regard to the book of Judges, I suppose no rational person persuades himself that it was written by the actual Judges. For the conclusion of the whole history contained in chap. ii. clearly shows that it is all the work—of a single historian. Further, inasmuch as the writer frequently tells us that there was then no king in Israel, it is evident that the book was written after the establishment of the monarchy.

The books of Samuel need not detain us long, inasmuch as the narrative in them is continued long after Samuel's death; but I should like to draw attention to the fact that it was written many generations after Samuel's death. For in book i. chap. ix:9, the historian remarks in a, parenthesis, "Beforetime, in Israel, when a man went to inquire of God, thus he spake: Come, and let us go to the seer; for he that is now called a prophet was beforetime called a seer."

Lastly, the books of Kings, as we gather from internal evidence, were compiled from the books of King Solomon (I Kings xi:41), from the chronicles of the kings of Judah (1 Kings xiv:19, 29), and the chronicles of the kings of Israel.

We may, therefore, conclude that all the books we have considered hitherto are compilations, and that the events therein are recorded as having happened in old time. Now, if we turn our attention to the connection and argument of all these books, we shall easily see that they were all written by a single historian, who wished to relate the antiquities of the Jews from their first beginning down to the first destruction of the city. The way in which the several books are connected one with the other is alone enough to show us that they form the narrative of one and the same writer. For as soon as he has related the life of Moses, the historian thus passes on to the story of Joshua: "And it came to pass after that Moses the servant of the Lord was dead, that God spake unto Joshua," &c., so in the same way, after the death of Joshua was concluded, he passes with identically the same transition and connection to the history of the Judges: "And it came to pass after that Joshua was dead, that the children of Israel sought from God," &c. To the book of Judges he adds the story of Ruth, as a sort of appendix, in these words: "Now it came to pass in the days that the judges ruled, that there was a famine in the land."

The first book of Samuel is introduced with a similar phrase; and so is the second book of Samuel. Then, before the history of David is concluded, the historian passes in the same way to the first book of Kings, and, after David's death, to the Second book of Kings.

The putting together, and the order of the narratives, show that they are all the work of one man, writing with a create aim; for the historian begins with relating the first origin of the Hebrew nation, and then sets forth in order the times and the occasions in which Moses put forth his laws, and made his predictions. He then proceeds to relate how the Israelites invaded the promised land in accordance with Moses' prophecy (Deut. vii.); and how, when the land was subdued, they turned their backs on their laws, and thereby incurred many misfortunes (Deut. xxxi:16, 17). He tells how they wished to elect rulers, and how, according as these rulers observed the law, the people flourished or suffered (Deut. xxviii:36); finally, how destruction came upon the nation, even as Moses had foretold. In regard to other matters, which do not serve to confirm the law, the writer either passes over them in silence, or refers the reader to other books for information. All that is set down in the books we have conduces to the sole object of setting forth the words and laws of Moses, and proving them by subsequent events.When we put together these three considerations, namely, the unity of the subject of all the books, the connection between them, and the fact that they are compilations made many generations after the events they relate had taken place, we come to the conclusion, as I have just stated, that they are all the work of a single historian. Who this historian was, it is not so easy to show; but I suspect that he was Ezra, and there are several strong reasons for adopting this hypothesis.

The historian whom we already know to be but one individual brings his history down to the liberation of Jehoiakim, and adds that he himself sat at the king's table all his life—that is, at the table either of Jehoiakim, or of the son of Nebuchadnezzar, for the sense of the passage is ambiguous: hence it follows that he did not live before the time of Ezra. But Scripture does not testify of any except of Ezra (Ezra vii:10), that he "prepared his heart to seek the law of the Lord, and to set it forth, and further that he was a ready scribe in the law of Moses." Therefore, I can not find anyone, save Ezra, to whom to attribute the sacred books.

Further, from this testimony concerning Ezra, we see that he prepared his heart, not only to seek the law of the Lord, but also to set it forth; and, in Nehemiah viii:8, we read that "they read in the book of the law of God distinctly, and gave the sense, and caused them to understand the reading."

As, then, in Deuteronomy, we find not only the book of the law of Moses, or the greater part of it, but also many things inserted for its better explanation, I conjecture that this Deuteronomy is the book of the law of God, written, set forth, and explained by Ezra, which is referred to in the text above quoted. Two examples of the way matters were inserted parenthetically in the text of Deuteronomy, with a view to its fuller explanation, we have already given, in speaking of Aben Ezra's opinion. Many others are found in the course of the work: for instance, in chap. ii:12: "The Horims dwelt also in Seir beforetime; but the children of Esau succeeded them, when they had destroyed them from before them, and dwelt in their stead; as Israel did unto the land of his possession, which the Lord gave unto them." This explains verses 3 and 4 of the same chapter, where it is stated that Mount Seir, which had come to the children of Esau for a possession, did not fall into their hands uninhabited; but that they invaded it, and turned out and destroyed the Horims, who formerly dwelt therein, even as the children of Israel had done unto the Canaanites after the death of Moses.

So, also, verses 6, 7, 8, 9, of the tenth chapter are inserted parenthetically among the words of Moses. Everyone must see that verse 8, which begins, "At that time the Lord separated the tribe of Levi," necessarily refers to verse 5, and not to the death of Aaron, which is only mentioned here by Ezra because Moses, in telling of the golden calf worshipped by the people, stated that he had prayed for Aaron.

He then explains that at the time at which Moses spoke, God had chosen for Himself the tribe of Levi in order that He may point out the reason for their election, and for the fact of their not sharing in the inheritance; after this digression, he resumes the thread of Moses' speech. To these parentheses we must add the preface to the book, and all the passages in which Moses is spoken of in the third person, besides many which we cannot now distinguish, though, doubtless, they would have been plainly recognized by the writer's contemporaries.

If, I say, we were in possession of the book of the law as Moses wrote it, I do not doubt that we should find a great difference in the words of the precepts, the order in which they are given, and the reasons by which they are supported.

A comparison of the decalogue in Deuteronomy with the decalogue in Exodus, where its history is explicitly set forth, will be sufficient to show us a wide discrepancy in all these three particulars, for the fourth commandment is given not only in a different form, but at much greater length, while the reason for its observance differs wholly from that stated in Exodus. Again, the order in which the tenth commandment is explained differs in the two versions. I think that the differences here as elsewhere are the work of Ezra, who explained the law of God to his contemporaries, and who wrote this book of the law of God, before anything else; this I gather from the fact that it contains the laws of the country, of which the people stood in most need, and also because it is not joined to the book which precedes it by any connecting phrase, but begins with the independent statement, "these are the words of Moses." After this task was completed, I think Ezra set himself to give a complete account of the history of the Hebrew nation from the creation of the world to the entire destruction of the city, and in this account he inserted the book of Deuteronomy, and, possibly, he called the first five books by the name of Moses, because his life is chiefly contained therein, and forms their principal subject; for the same reason he called the sixth Joshua, the seventh Judges, the eighth Ruth, the ninth, and perhaps the tenth, Samuel, and, lastly, the eleventh and twelfth Kings. Whether Ezra put the finishing touches to this work and finished it as he intended, we will discuss in the next chapter.

CHAPTER IX

Other Questions Concerning the Same Books:
Namely, Whether They Were Completely Finished by Ezra,
And, Further, Whether the Marginal Notes Which are
Found in the Hebrew Texts Were Various Readings.

HOW greatly the inquiry we have just made concerning the real writer of the twelve books aids us in attaining a complete understanding of them, may be easily gathered solely from the passages which we have adduced in confirmation of our opinion, and which would be most obscure without it. But besides the question of the writer, there are other points to notice which common superstition forbids the multitude to apprehend. Of these the chief is, that Ezra (whom I will take to be the author of the aforesaid books until some more likely person be suggested) did not put the finishing touches to the narrative contained therein, but merely collected the histories from various writers, and sometimes simply set them down, leaving their examination and arrangement to posterity.

The cause (if it were not untimely death) which prevented him from completing his work in all its portions, I cannot conjecture, but the fact remains most clear, although we have lost the writings of the ancient Hebrew historians, and can only judge from the few fragments which are still extant. For the history of Hezekiah (2 Kings xviii:17), as written in the vision of Isaiah, is related as it is found in the chronicles of the kings of Judah. We read the same story, told with few exceptions,[6] in the same words, in the book of Isaiah which was contained in the chronicles of the kings of Judah (2 Chron. xxxii:32). From this we must conclude that there were various versions

---

6   See Endnote 11.

of this narrative of Isaiah's, unless, indeed, anyone would dream that in this, too, there lurks a mystery. Further, the last chapter of 2 Kings 27-30 is repeated in the last chapter of Jeremiah, v.31-34.

Again, we find 2 Sam. vii. repeated in I Chron. xvii., but the expressions in the two passages are so curiously varied,[7] that we can very easily see that these two chapters were taken from two different versions of the history of Nathan.

Lastly, the genealogy of the kings of Idumaea contained in Genesis xxxvi:31, is repeated in the same words in 1 Chron. i., though we know that the author of the latter work took his materials from other historians, not from the twelve books we have ascribed to Ezra. We may therefore be sure that if we still possessed the writings of the historians, the matter would be made clear; however, as we have lost them, we can only examine the writings still extant, and from their order and connection, their various repetitions, and, lastly, the contradictions in dates which they contain, judge of the rest.

These, then, or the chief of them, we will now go through. First, in the story of Judah and Tamar (Gen. xxxviii.) the historian thus begins: "And it came to pass at that time that Judah went down from his brethren." This time cannot refer to what immediately precedes,[8] but must necessarily refer to something else, for from the time when Joseph was sold into Egypt to the time when the patriarch Jacob, with all his family, set out thither, cannot be reckoned as more than twenty-two years, for Joseph, when he was sold by his brethren, was seventeen years old, and when he was summoned by Pharaoh from prison was thirty; if to this we add the seven years of plenty and two of famine, the total amounts to twenty-two years. Now, in so short a period, no one can suppose that so many things happened as are described; that Judah had three children, one after the other, from one wife, whom he married at the beginning of the period; that the eldest of these, when he was old enough, married Tamar, and that after he died his next

---

7   See Endnote 12.
8   See Endnote 13.

brother succeeded to her; that, after all this, Judah, without knowing it, had intercourse with his daughter-in-law, and that she bore him twins, and, finally, that the eldest of these twins became a father within the aforesaid period. As all these events cannot have taken place within the period mentioned in Genesis, the reference must necessarily be to something treated of in another book: and Ezra in this instance simply related the story, and inserted it without examination among his other writings.

However, not only this chapter but the whole narrative of Joseph and Jacob is collected and set forth from various histories, inasmuch as it is quite inconsistent with itself. For in Gen. xlvii. we are told that Jacob, when he came at Joseph's bidding to salute Pharaoh, was 130 years old. If from this we deduct the twenty-two years which he passed sorrowing for the absence of Joseph and the seventeen years forming Joseph's age when he was sold, and, lastly, the seven years for which Jacob served for Rachel, we find that he was very advanced in life, namely, eighty four, when he took Leah to wife, whereas Dinah was scarcely seven years old when she was violated by Shechem.[9] Simeon and Levi were aged respectively eleven and twelve when they spoiled the city and slew all the males therein with the sword.

There is no need that I should go through the whole Pentateuch. If anyone pays attention to the way in which all the histories and precepts in these five books are set down promiscuously and without order, with no regard for dates; and further, how the same story is often repeated, sometimes in a different version, he will easily, I say, discern that all the materials were promiscuously collected and heaped together, in order that they might at some subsequent time be more readily examined and reduced to order. Not only these five books, but also the narratives contained in the remaining seven, going down to the destruction of the city, are compiled in the same way. For who does not see that in Judges ii:6 a new historian is being quoted, who had also written of the deeds of Joshua, and that his words are simply copied? For after our historian has

9   See Endnote 14.

stated in the last chapter of the book of Joshua that Joshua died and was buried, and has promised, in the first chapter of Judges, to relate what happened after his death, in what way, if he wished to continue the thread of his history, could he connect the statement here made about Joshua with what had gone before?

So, too, 1 Sam. 17, 18, are taken from another historian, who assigns a cause for David's first frequenting Saul's court very different from that given in chap. xvi. of the same book. For he did not think that David came to Saul in consequence of the advice of Saul's servants, as is narrated in chap. xvi., but that being sent by chance to the camp by his father on a message to his brothers, he was for the first time remarked by Saul on the occasion of his victory, over Goliath the Philistine, and was retained at his court.

I suspect the same thing has taken place in chap. xxvi. of the same book, for the historian there seems to repeat the narrative given in chap. xxiv. according to another man's version. But I pass over this, and go on to the computation of dates.

In I Kings, chap. vi., it is said that Solomon built the Temple in the four hundred and eightieth year after the exodus from Egypt; but from the historians themselves we get a much longer period, for:

YEARS.

Moses governed the people in the desert 40
Joshua, who lived 110 years, did not, according to
Josephus and others' opinion rule more than......................26
Cusban Rishathaim held the people in subjection 8
Othniel, son of Kenag, was judge for...............................[10]40
Eglon, King of Moab, governed the people........................... 18
Ehucl and Shamgar were judges..80
Jachin, King of Canaan, held the people in subjection.........20
The people was at peace subsequently for...........................40

---

10   See Endnote 15.

All these periods added together make a total of 580 years. But to these must be added the years during which the Hebrew republic flourished after the death of Joshua, until it was conquered by Cushan Rishathaim, which I take to be very numerous, for I cannot bring myself to believe that immediately after the death of Joshua all those who had witnessed his miracles died simultaneously, nor that their successors at one stroke bid farewell to their laws, and plunged from the highest virtue into the depth of wickedness and obstinacy.

Nor, lastly, that Cushan Rishathaim subdued them on the instant; each one of these circumstances requires almost a generation, and there is no doubt that Judges ii:7, 9, 10, comprehends a great many years which it passes over in silence. We must also add the years during which Samuel was judge, the number of which is not stated in Scripture, and also the years during which Saul reigned, which are not clearly shown from

11   See Endnote 16.

his history. It is, indeed, stated in 1 Sam. xiii:1, that he reigned two years, but the text in that passage is mutilated, and the records of his reign lead us to suppose a longer period. That the text is mutilated I suppose no one will doubt who has ever advanced so far as the threshold of the Hebrew language, for it runs as follows: "Saul was in his—year, when he began to reign, and he reigned two years over Israel." Who, I say, does not see that the number of the years of Saul's age when he began to reign has been omitted? That the record of the reign presupposes a greater number of years is equally beyond doubt, for in the same book, chap. xxvii:7, it is stated that David sojourned among the Philistines, to whom he had fled on account of Saul, a year and four months; thus the rest of the reign must have been comprised in a space of eight months, which I think no one will credit. Josephus, at the end of the sixth book of his antiquities, thus corrects the text: Saul reigned eighteen years while Samuel was alive, and two years after his death. However, all the narrative in chap. Xiii. is in complete disagreement with what goes before. At the end of chap. vii. it is narrated that the Philistines were so crushed by the Hebrews that they did not venture, during Samuel's life, to invade the borders of Israel; but in chap. xiii. we are told that the Hebrews were invaded during the life of Samuel by the Philistines, and reduced by them to such a state of wretchedness and poverty that they were deprived not only of weapons with which to defend themselves, but also of the means of making more. I should be at pains enough if I were to try and harmonize all the narratives contained in this first book of Samuel so that they should seem to be all written and arranged by a single historian. But I return to my object. The years, then, during which Saul reigned must be added to the above computation; and, lastly, I have not counted the years of the Hebrew anarchy, for I cannot from Scripture gather their number. I cannot, I say, be certain as to the period occupied by the events related in Judges chap. xvii. on till the end of the book.

It is thus abundantly evident that we cannot arrive at a true computation of years from the histories, and, further, that the histories are inconsistent themselves on the subject. We are compelled to confess that these histories were compiled from various writers without previous arrangement and examination. Not less discrepancy is found between the dates given in the Chronicles of the Kings of Judah, and those in the Chronicles of the Kings of Israel; in the latter, it is stated that Jehoram, the son of Ahab, began to reign in the second year of the reign of Jehoram, the son of Jehoshaphat (2 Kings i:17), but in the former we read that Jehoram, the son of Jehoshaphat, began to reign in the fifth year of Jehoram, the son of Ahab (2 Kings viii:16). Anyone who compares the narratives in Chronicles with the narratives in the books of Kings, will find many similar discrepancies. These there is no need for me to examine here, and still less am I called upon to treat of the commentaries of those who endeavour to harmonize them. The Rabbis evidently let their fancy run wild. Such commentators as I have, read, dream, invent, and as a last resort, play fast and loose with the language. For instance, when it is said in 2 Chronicles, that Ahab was forty-two years old when he began to reign, they pretend that these years are computed from the reign of Omri, not from the birth of Ahab. If this can be shown to be the real meaning of the writer of the book of Chronicles, all I can say is, that he did not know how to state a fact. The commentators make many other assertions of this kind, which if true, would prove that the ancient Hebrews were ignorant both of their own language, and of the way to relate a plain narrative. I should in such case recognize no rule or reason in interpreting Scripture, but it would be permissible to hypothesize to one's heart's content.

If anyone thinks that I am speaking too generally, and without sufficient warrant, I would ask him to set himself to showing us some fixed plan in these histories which might be followed without blame by other writers of chronicles, and in his efforts at harmonizing and interpretation, so strictly to observe and explain the phrases and expressions, the order and the connections, that we may be able to imitate these also in our writings.[12] If he succeeds, I will at once give him my hand, and he shall be to me as great Apollo; for I confess that after long endeavours I have been unable to discover anything

12   See Endnote 17.

of the kind. I may add that I set down nothing here which I have not long reflected upon, and that, though I was imbued from my boyhood up with the ordinary opinions about the Scriptures, I have been unable to withstand the force of what I have urged.

However, there is no need to detain the reader with this question, and drive him to attempt an impossible task; I merely mentioned the fact in order to throw light on my intention.

I now pass on to other points concerning the treatment of these books. For we must remark, in addition to what has been shown, that these books were not guarded by posterity with such care that no faults crept in. The ancient scribes draw attention to many doubtful readings, and some mutilated passages, but not to all that exist: whether the faults are of sufficient importance to greatly embarrass the reader I will not now discuss. I am inclined to think that they are of minor moment to those, at any rate, who read the Scriptures with enlightenment: and I can positively, affirm that I have not noticed any fault or various reading in doctrinal passages sufficient to render them obscure or doubtful.

There are some people, however, who will not admit that there is any corruption, even in other passages, but maintain that by some unique exercise of providence God has preserved from corruption every word in the Bible: they say that the various readings are the symbols of profoundest mysteries, and that mighty secrets lie hid in the twenty-eight hiatus which occur, nay, even in the very form of the letters.

Whether they are actuated by folly and anile devotion, or whether by arrogance and malice so that they alone may be held to possess the secrets of God, I know not: this much I do know, that I find in their writings nothing which has the air of a Divine secret, but only childish lucubrations. I have read and known certain Kabbalistic triflers, whose insanity provokes my unceasing as astonishment. That faults have crept in will, I think, be denied by no sensible person who reads the passage about Saul, above quoted (1 Sam. xiii:1) and also 2 Sam. vi:2:

"And David arose and went with all the people that were with him from Judah, to bring up from thence the ark of God."

No one can fail to remark that the name of their destination, viz., Kirjath-jearim,[13] has been omitted: nor can we deny that 2 Sam. xiii:37, has been tampered with and mutilated. "And Absalom fled, and went to Talmai, the son of Ammihud, king of Geshur. And he mourned for his son every day. So Absalom fled, and went to Geshur, and was there three years." I know that I have remarked other passages of the same kind, but I cannot recall them at the moment.

That the marginal notes which are found continually in the Hebrew Codices are doubtful readings will, I think, be evident to everyone who has noticed that they often arise from the great similarity, of some of the Hebrew letters, such for instance, as the similarity between Kaph and Beth, Jod and Van, Daleth and Reth, &c. For example, the text in 2 Sam. v:24, runs "in the time when thou hearest," and similarly in Judges xxi:22, "And it shall be when their fathers or their brothers come unto us often," the marginal version is "come unto us to complain."

So also many various readings have arisen from the use of the letters named mutes, which are generally not sounded in pronunciation, and are taken promiscuously, one for the other. For example, in Levit. xxv:29, it is written, "The house shall be established which is not in the walled city," but the margin has it, "which is in a walled city."

Though these matters are self-evident, [Endnore 6], it is necessary, to answer the reasonings of certain Pharisees, by which they endeavour to convince us that the marginal notes serve to indicate some mystery, and were added or pointed out by the writers of the sacred books. The first of these reasons, which, in my, opinion, carries little weight, is taken from the practice of reading the Scriptures aloud.

If, it is urged, these notes were added to show various readings which could not be decided upon by posterity, why has custom prevailed that the marginal readings should always be

13   See Endnote 18.

retained? Why has the meaning which is preferred been set down in the margin when it ought to have been incorporated in the text, and not relegated to a side note?

The second reason is more specious, and is taken from the nature of the case. It is admitted that faults have crept into the sacred writings by chance and not by design; but they say that in the five books the word for a girl is, with one exception, written without the letter "he," contrary to all grammatical rules, whereas in the margin it is written correctly according to the universal rule of grammar. Can this have happened by mistake? Is it possible to imagine a clerical error to have been committed every, time the word occurs? Moreover, it would have been easy, to supply the emendation. Hence, when these readings are not accidental or corrections of manifest mistakes, it is supposed that they must have been set down on purpose by the original writers, and have a meaning. However, it is easy to answer such arguments; as to the question of custom having prevailed in the reading of the marginal versions, I will not spare much time for its consideration: I know not the promptings of superstition, and perhaps the practice may have arisen from the idea that both readings were deemed equally good or tolerable, and therefore, lest either should be neglected, one was appointed to be written, and the other to be read. They feared to pronounce judgment in so weighty a matter lest they should mistake the false for the true, and therefore they would give preference to neither, as they must necessarily have done if they had commanded one only to be both read and written. This would be especially the case where the marginal readings were not written down in the sacred books: or the custom may have originated because some things though rightly written down were desired to be read otherwise according to the marginal version, and therefore the general rule was made that the marginal version should be followed in reading the Scriptures. The cause which induced the scribes to expressly prescribe certain passages to be read in the marginal version, I will now touch on, for not all the marginal notes are various readings, but some mark expressions which have passed out of common use, obsolete words and terms which current decency did not allow to be read in a public assembly. The ancient writers, without any evil intention, employed no courtly paraphrase, but called things by their plain names. (891) Afterwards, through the spread of evil thoughts and luxury, words which could be used by the ancients without offence, came to be considered obscene. There was no need for this cause to change the text of Scripture. Still, as a concession to the popular weakness, it became the custom to substitute more decent terms for words denoting sexual intercourse, exereta, &c., and to read them as they were given in the margin.

At any rate, whatever may have been the origin of the practice of reading Scripture according to the marginal version, it was not that the true interpretation is contained therein. For besides that, the Rabbins in the Talmud often differ from the Massoretes, and give other readings which they approve of, as I will shortly show, certain things are found in the margin which appear less warranted by the uses of the Hebrew language. For example, in 2 Samuel xiv:22, we read, "In that the king hath fulfilled the request of his servant," a construction plainly regular, and agreeing with that in chap. xvi. But the margin has it "of thy servant," which does not agree with the person of the verb. So, too, chap. xvi:25 of the same book, we find, "As if one had inquired at the oracle of God," the margin adding "someone" to stand as a nominative to the verb. But the correction is not apparently warranted, for it is a common practice, well known to grammarians in the Hebrew language, to use the third person singular of the active verb impersonally.

The second argument advanced by the Pharisees is easily answered from what has just been said, namely, that the scribes besides the various readings called attention to obsolete words. For there is no doubt that in Hebrew as in other languages, changes of use made many words obsolete and antiquated, and such were found by the later scribes in the sacred books and noted by them with a view to the books being publicly read according to custom. For this reason the word nahgar is always found marked because its gender was originally common, and it had the same meaning as the Latin juvenis (a young person).

So also the Hebrew capital was anciently called Jerusalem, not Jerusalaim. As to the pronouns himself and herself, I think that the later scribes changed vau into jod (a very frequent change in Hebrew) when they wished to express the feminine gender, but that the ancients only distinguished the two genders by a change of vowels. I may also remark that the irregular tenses of certain verbs differ in the ancient and modern forms, it being formerly considered a mark of elegance to employ certain letters agreeable to the ear.

In a word, I could easily multiply proofs of this kind if I were not afraid of abusing the patience of the reader. Perhaps I shall be asked how I became acquainted with the fact that all these expressions are obsolete. I reply that I have found them in the most ancient Hebrew writers in the Bible itself, and that they have not been imitated by subsequent authors, and thus they are recognized as antiquated, though the language in which they occur is dead. But perhaps someone may press the question why, if it be true, as I say, that the marginal notes of the Bible generally mark various readings, there are never more than two readings of a passage, that in the text and that in the margin, instead of three or more; and further, how the scribes can have hesitated between two readings, one of which is evidently contrary to grammar, and the other a plain correction.

The answer to these questions also is easy: I will premise that it is almost certain that there once were more various readings than those now recorded. For instance, one finds many in the Talmud which the Massoretes have neglected, and are so different one from the other that even the superstitious editor of the Bomberg Bible confesses that he cannot harmonize them. "We cannot say anything," he writes, "except what we have said above, namely, that the Talmud is generally in contradiction to the Massorete." So that we are nor bound to hold that there never were more than two readings of any passage, yet I am willing to admit, and indeed I believe that more than two readings are never found: and for the following reasons:-(I.) The cause of the differences of reading only admits of two, being generally the similarity of certain letters, so that the question resolved itself into which should be written Beth, or Kaf, Jod or Vau, Daleth or Reth: cases which are constantly occurring, and frequently yielding a fairly good meaning whichever alternative be adopted. Sometimes, too, it is a question whether a syllable be long or short, quantity being determined by the letters called mutes. Moreover, we never asserted that all the marginal versions, without exception, marked various readings; on the contrary, we have stated that many were due to motives of decency or a desire to explain obsolete words. (II.) I am inclined to attribute the fact that more than two readings are never found to the paucity of exemplars, perhaps not more than two or three, found by the scribes. In the treatise of the scribes, chap. vi., mention is made of three only, pretended to have been found in the time of Ezra, in order that the marginal versions might be attributed to him.

However that may be, if the scribes only had three codices we may easily imagine that in a given passage two of them would be in accord, for it would be extraordinary if each one of the three gave a different reading of the same text.

The dearth of copies after the time of Ezra will surprise no one who has read the 1st chapter of Maccabees, or Josephus's "Antiquities," Bk. 12, chap. 5. Nay, it appears wonderful considering the fierce and daily persecution, that even these few should have been preserved. This will, I think, be plain to even a cursory reader of the history of those times.

We have thus discovered the reasons why there are never more than two readings of a passage in the Bible, but this is a long way from supposing that we may therefore conclude that the Bible was purposely written incorrectly in such passages in order to signify some mystery. As to the second argument, that some passages are so faultily written that they are at plain variance with all grammar, and should have been corrected in the text and not in the margin, I attach little weight to it, for I am not concerned to say what religious motive the scribes may have had for acting as they did: possibly they did so from candour, wishing to transmit the few exemplars of the Bible which they had found exactly in their original state, marking the differences they discovered in the margin, not as doubtful readings, but as simple variants. I have myself called them doubtful readings, because it would be generally impossible to say which of the two versions is preferable.

Lastly, besides these doubtful readings the scribes have (by leaving a hiatus in the middle of a paragraph) marked several passages as mutilated. The Massoretes have counted up such instances, and they amount to eight-and-twenty. I do not know whether any mystery is thought to lurk in the number, at any rate the Pharisees religiously preserve a certain amount of empty space.

One of such hiatus occurs (to give an instance) in Gen. iv:8, where it is written, "And Cain said to his brother . . . . and it came to pass while they were in the field, &c.," a space being left in which we should expect to hear what it was that Cain said.

Similarly there are (besides those points we have noticed) eight-and-twenty hiatus left by the scribes. Many of these would not be recognized as mutilated if it were not for the empty space left. But I have said enough on this subject.

CHAPTER X

An Examination of the Remaining Books of the Old Testament According to the Preceding Method.

I now pass on to the remaining books of the Old Testament. Concerning the two books of Chronicles I have nothing particular or important to remark, except that they were certainly written after the time of Ezra, and possibly after the restoration of the Temple by Judas Maccabaeus.[14] For in chap. ix. of the first book we find a reckoning of the families who were the first to live in Jerusalem, and in verse 17 the names of the porters, of which two recur in Nehemiah. This shows that the books were certainly compiled after the rebuilding of the city. As to their actual writer, their authority, utility, and doctrine, I come to no conclusion. I have always been astonished that they have been included in the Bible by men who shut out from the canon the books of Wisdom, Tobit, and the others styled apocryphal. I do not aim at disparaging their authority, but as they are universally received I will leave them as they are.

The Psalms were collected and divided into five books in the time of the second temple, for Ps. lxxxviii. was published, according to Philo-Judaeus, while king Jehoiachin was still a prisoner in Babylon; and Ps. lxxxix. when the same king obtained his liberty: I do not think Philo would have made the statement unless either it had been the received opinion in his time, or else had been told him by trustworthy persons.

The Proverbs of Solomon were, I believe, collected at the same time, or at least in the time of King Josiah; for in chap. xxv:1,

14   See Endnote 19.

it is written, "These are also proverbs of Solomon which the men of Hezekiah, king of Judah, copied out." I cannot here pass over in silence the audacity of the Rabbis who wished to exclude from the sacred canon both the Proverbs and Ecclesiastes, and to put them both in the Apocrypha. In fact, they would actually have done so, if they had not lighted on certain passages in which the law of Moses is extolled. It is, indeed, grievous to think that the settling of the sacred canon lay in the hands of such men; however, I congratulate them, in this instance, on their suffering us to see these books in question, though I cannot refrain from doubting whether they have transmitted them in absolute good faith; but I will not now linger on this point.

I pass on, then, to the prophetic books. An examination of these assures me that the prophecies therein contained have been compiled from other books, and are not always set down in the exact order in which they were spoken or written by the prophets, but are only such as were collected here and there, so that they are but fragmentary.

Isaiah began to prophecy in the reign of Uzziah, as the writer himself testifies in the first verse. He not only prophesied at that time, but furthermore wrote the history of that king (see 2 Chron. xxvi:22) in a volume now lost. That which we possess, we have shown to have been taken from the chronicles of the kings of Judah and Israel.

We may add that the Rabbis assert that this prophet prophesied in the reign of Manasseh, by whom he was eventually put to death, and, although this seems to be a myth, it yet shows that they did not think that all Isaiah's prophecies are extant.

The prophecies of Jeremiah, which are related historically are also taken from various chronicles; for not only are they heaped together confusedly, without any account being taken of dates, but also the same story is told in them differently in different passages. For instance, in chap. xxi. we are told that the cause of Jeremiah's arrest was that he had prophesied the destruction of the city to Zedekiah who consulted him. This

narrative suddenly passes, in chap xxii., to the prophet's re-
monstrances to Jehoiakim (Zedekiah's predecessor), and the
prediction he made of that king's captivity; then, in chap. xxv.,
come the revelations granted to the prophet previously, that is
in the fourth year of Jehoiakim, and, further on still, the revelations received in the first year of the same reign. The con-
tinuator of Jeremiah goes on heaping prophecy upon prophecy
without any regard to dates, until at last, in chap. xxxviii. (as if
the intervening chapters had been a parenthesis), he takes up
the thread dropped in chap. xxi.

In fact, the conjunction with which chap. xxxviii. begins, refers
to the 8th, 9th, and 10th verses of chap. xxi. Jeremiah's last arrest is then very differently described, and a totally separate
cause is given for his daily retention in the court of the prison.

We may thus clearly see that these portions of the book have
been compiled from various sources, and are only from this
point of view comprehensible. The prophecies contained in the
remaining chapters, where Jeremiah speaks in the first person,
seem to be taken from a book written by Baruch, at Jeremiah's
dictation. These, however, only comprise (as appears from
chap. xxxvi:2) the prophecies revealed to the prophet from the
time of Josiah to the fourth year of Jehoiakim, at which period
the book begins. The contents of chap. xlv:2, on to chap. li:59,
seem taken from the same volume.

That the book of Ezekiel is only a fragment, is clearly indi-
cated by the first verse. For anyone may see that the conjunction with which it begins, refers to something already said,
and connects what follows therewith. However, not only this
conjunction, but the whole text of the discourse implies other
writings. The fact of the present work beginning the thirtieth
year shows that the prophet is continuing, not commencing a
discourse; and this is confirmed by the writer, who parenthetically states in verse 3, "The word of the Lord came often unto
Ezekiel the priest, the son of Buzi, in the land of the Chaldeans,"
as if to say that the prophecies which he is about to relate are
the sequel to revelations formerly received by Ezekiel from
God. Furthermore, Josephus, 11 Antiq." x:9, says that Ezekiel

prophesied that Zedekiah should not see Babylon, whereas the book we now have not only contains no such statement, but contrariwise asserts in chap. xvii. that he should be taken to Babylon as a captive.[15]

Of Hosea I cannot positively state that he wrote more than is now extant in the book bearing his name, but I am astonished at the smallness of the quantity, we possess, for the sacred writer asserts that the prophet prophesied for more than eighty years.

We may assert, speaking generally, that the compiler of the prophetic books neither collected all the prophets, nor all the writings of those we have; for of the prophets who are said to have prophesied in the reign of Manasseh and of whom general mention is made in 2 Chron. xxxiii:10, 18, we have, evidently, no prophecies extant; neither have we all the prophecies of the twelve who give their names to books. Of Jonah we have only, the prophecy concerning the Ninevites, though he also prophesied to the children of Israel, as we learn in 2 Kings xiv:25.

The book and the personality of Job have caused much controversy. Some think that the book is the work of Moses, and the whole narrative merely allegorical. Such is the opinion of the Rabbins recorded in the Talmud, and they are supported by, Maimonides in his "More Nebuchim." Others believe it to be a true history, and some suppose that Job lived in the time of Jacob, and was married to his daughter Dinah. Aben Ezra, however, as I have already stated, affirms, in his commentaries, that the work is a translation into Hebrew from some other language: I could wish that he could advance more cogent arguments than he does, for we might then conclude that the Gentiles also had sacred books. I myself leave the matter undecided, but I conjecture Job to have been a Gentile, and a man of very stable character, who at first prospered, then was assailed with terrible calamities, and finally, was restored to great happiness. (He is thus named, among others, by Ezekiel, xiv:12.) I take it that the constancy of his mind amid the vicissitudes of his fortune occasioned many men to dispute about

15   See Endnote 20.

God's providence, or at least caused the writer of the book in question to compose his dialogues; for the contents, and also the style, seem to emanate far less from a man wretchedly ill and lying among ashes, than from one reflecting at ease in his study. I should also be inclined to agree with Aben Ezra that the book is a translation, for its poetry seems akin to that of the Gentiles; thus the Father of Gods summons a council, and Momus, here called Satan, criticizes the Divine decrees with the utmost freedom. But these are mere conjectures without any solid foundation.

I pass on to the book of Daniel, which, from chap. viii. onwards, undoubtedly contains the writing of Daniel himself. Whence the first seven chapters are derived I cannot say; we may, however, conjecture that, as they were first written in Chaldean, they are taken from Chaldean chronicles. If this could be proved, it would form a very striking proof of the fact that the sacredness of Scripture depends on our understanding of the doctrines therein signified, and not on the words, the language, and the phrases in which these doctrines are conveyed to us; and it would further show us that books which teach and speak of whatever is highest and best are equally sacred, whatever be the tongue in which they are written, or the nation to which they belong.

We can, however, in this case only remark that the chapters in question were written in Chaldee, and yet are as sacred as the rest of the Bible.

The first book of Ezra is so intimately connected with the book of Daniel that both are plainly recognizable as the work of the same author, writing of Jewish history from the time of the first captivity onwards. I have no hesitation in joining to this the book of Esther, for the conjunction with which it begins can refer to nothing else. It cannot be the same work as that written by Mordecai, for, in chap. ix:20-22, another person relates that Mordecai wrote letters, and tells us their contents; further, that Queen Esther confirmed the days of Purim in their times appointed, and that the decree was written in the book that is (by a Hebraism), in a book known to all then living, which, as Aben Ezra and the rest confess, has now perished. Lastly, for the rest of the acts of Morde-cai, the historian refers us to the chronicles of the kings of Persia. Thus there is no doubt that this book was written by the same person as he who recounted the history of Dan-iel and Ezra, and who wrote Nehemiah,[16] sometimes called the second book of Ezra. We may, then, affirm that all these books are from one hand; but we have no clue whatever to the personality of the author. However, in order to deter-mine whence he, whoever he was, had gained a knowledge of the histories which he had, perchance, in great measure himself written, we may remark that the governors or chiefs of the Jews, after the restoration of the Temple, kept scribes or historiographers, who wrote annals or chronicles of them. The chronicles of the kings are often quoted in the books of Kings, but the chronicles of the chiefs and priests are quoted for the first time in Nehemiah xii:23, and again in 1 Macc. xvi:24. This is undoubtedly the book referred to as contain-ing the decree of Esther and the acts of Mordecai; and which, as we said with Aben Ezra, is now lost. From it were taken the whole contents of these four books, for no other author-ity is quoted by their writer, or is known to us.

That these books were not written by either Ezra or Nehemiah is plain from Nehemiah xii:9, where the descendants of the high priest, Joshua are traced down to Jaddua, the sixth high priest, who went to meet Alexander the Great, when the Persian empire was almost subdued (Josephus, "Ant." ii. 108), or who, according to Philo-Judaeus, was the sixth and last high priest under the Persians. In the same chapter of Nehemiah, verse 22, this point is clearly brought out: "The Levites in the days of Eliashib, Joiada, and Johanan, and Jaddua, were record-ed chief of the fathers: also the priests, to the reign of Darius the Persian"—that is to say, in the chronicles; and, I suppose, no one thinks,[17] that the lives of Nehemiah and Ezra were so prolonged that they outlived fourteen kings of Persia. Cyrus was the first who granted the Jews permission to rebuild their Temple: the period between his time and Darius, fourteenth

16   See Endnote 21.
17   See Endnote 22.

and last king of Persia, extends over 230 years. I have, therefore, no doubt that these books were written after Judas Maccabaeus had restored the worship in the Temple, for at that time false books of Daniel, Ezra, and Esther were published by evil-disposed persons, who were almost certainly Sadducees, for the writings were never recognized by the Pharisees, so far as I am aware; and, although certain myths in the fourth book of Ezra are repeated in the Talmud, they must not be set down to the Pharisees, for all but the most ignorant admit that they have been added by some trifler: in fact, I think, someone must have made such additions with a view to casting ridicule on all the traditions of the sect.

Perhaps these four books were written out and published at the time I have mentioned with a view to showing the people that the prophecies of Daniel had been fulfilled, and thus kindling their piety, and awakening a hope of future deliverance in the midst of their misfortunes. In spite of their recent origin, the books before us contain many errors, due, I suppose, to the haste with which they were written. Marginal readings, such as I have mentioned in the last chapter, are found here as elsewhere, and in even greater abundance; there are, moreover, certain passages which can only be accounted for by supposing some such cause as hurry.

However, before calling attention to the marginal readings, I will remark that, if the Pharisees are right in supposing them to have been ancient, and the work of the original scribes, we must perforce admit that these scribes (if there were more than one) set them down because they found that the text from which they were copying was inaccurate, and did yet not venture to alter what was written by their predecessors and superiors. I need not again go into the subject at length, and will, therefore, proceed to mention some discrepancies not noticed in the margin.

I. Some error has crept into the text of the second chapter of Ezra, for in verse 64 we are told that the total of all those mentioned in the rest of the chapter amounts to 42,360; but, when we come to add up the several items we get as result only 29,818. There must, therefore, be an error, either in the total, or in the details. The total is probably correct, for it would most likely be well known to all as a noteworthy thing; but with the details, the case would be different. If, then, any error had crept into the total, it would at once have been remarked, and easily corrected. This view is confirmed by Nehemiah vii., where this chapter of Ezra is mentioned, and a total is given in plain correspondence thereto; but the details are altogether different—some are larger, and some less, than those in Ezra, and altogether they amount to 31,089. We may, therefore, conclude that both in Ezra and in Nehemiah the details are erroneously given. The commentators who attempt to harmonize these evident contradictions draw on their imagination, each to the best of his ability; and while professing adoration for each letter and word of Scripture, only succeed in holding up the sacred writers to ridicule, as though they knew not how to write or relate a plain narrative. Such persons effect nothing but to render the clearness of Scripture obscure. If the Bible could everywhere be interpreted after their fashion, there would be no such thing as a rational statement of which the meaning could be relied on. However, there is no need to dwell on the subject; only I am convinced that if any historian were to attempt to imitate the proceedings freely attributed to the writers of the Bible, the commentators would cover him with contempt. If it be blasphemy to assert that there are any errors in Scripture, what name shall we apply to those who foist into it their own fancies, who degrade the sacred writers till they seem to write confused nonsense, and who deny the plainest and most evident meanings? What in the whole Bible can be plainer than the fact that Ezra and his companions, in the second chapter of the book attributed to him, have given in detail the reckoning of all the Hebrews who set out with them for Jerusalem? This is proved by the reckoning being given, not only of those who told their lineage, but also of those who were unable to do so. Is it not equally clear from Nehemiah vii:5, that the writer merely there copies the list given in Ezra? Those, therefore, who explain these pas sages otherwise, deny the plain meaning of Scripture—nay, they deny Scripture itself.

They think it pious to reconcile one passage of Scripture with another—a pretty piety, forsooth, which accommodates the clear passages to the obscure, the correct to the faulty, the sound to the corrupt.

Far be it from me to call such commentators blasphemers, if their motives be pure: for to err is human. But I return to my subject.

Besides these errors in numerical details, there are others in the genealogies, in the history, and, I fear also in the prophecies. The prophecy of Jeremiah (chap. xxii.), concerning Jechoniah, evidently does not agree with his history, as given in I Chronicles iii:17-19, and especially with the last words of the chapter, nor do I see how the prophecy, "thou shalt die in peace," can be applied to Zedekiah, whose eyes were dug out after his sons had been slain before him. If prophecies are to be interpreted by their issue, we must make a change of name, and read Jechoniah for Zedekiah, and vice versa This, however, would be too paradoxical a proceeding; so I prefer to leave the matter unexplained, especially as the error, if error there be, must be set down to the historian, and not to any fault in the authorities.

Other difficulties I will not touch upon, as I should only weary the reader, and, moreover, be repeating the remarks of other writers. For R. Selomo, in face of the manifest contradiction in the above-mentioned genealogies, is compelled to break forth into these words (see his commentary on 1 Chron. viii.): "Ezra (whom he supposes to be the author of the book of Chronicles) gives different names and a different genealogy to the sons of Benjamin from those which we find in Genesis, and describes most of the Levites differently from Joshua, because he found original discrepancies." And, again, a little later: "The genealogy of Gibeon and others is described twice in different ways, from different tables of each genealogy, and in writing them down Ezra adopted the version given in the majority of the texts, and when the authority was equal he gave both." Thus granting that these books were compiled from sources originally incorrect and uncertain.

In fact the commentators, in seeking to harmonize difficulties, generally do no more than indicate their causes: for I suppose no sane person supposes that the sacred historians deliberately wrote with the object of appearing to contradict themselves freely. Perhaps I shall be told that I am overthrowing the authority of Scripture, for that, according to me, anyone may suspect it of error in any passage; but, on the contrary, I have shown that my object has been to prevent the clear and uncorrupted passages being accommodated to and corrupted by the faulty ones; neither does the fact that some passages are corrupt warrant us in suspecting all. No book ever was completely free from faults, yet I would ask, who suspects all books to be everywhere faulty? Surely no one, especially when the phraseology is clear and the intention of the author plain.

I have now finished the task I set myself with respect to the books of the Old Testament. We may easily conclude from what has been said, that before the time of the Maccabees there was no canon of sacred books,[18] but that those which we now possess were selected from a multitude of others at the period of the restoration of the Temple by the Pharisees (who also instituted the set form of prayers), who are alone responsible for their acceptance. Those, therefore, who would demonstrate the authority of Holy Scripture, are bound to show the authority of each separate book; it is not enough to prove the Divine origin of a single book in order to infer the Divine origin of the rest. In that case we should have to assume that the council of Pharisees was, in its choice of books, infallible, and this could never be proved. I am led to assert that the Pharisees alone selected the books of the Old Testament, and inserted them in the canon, from the fact that in Daniel ii. is proclaimed the doctrine of the Resurrection, which the Sadducees denied; and, furthermore, the Pharisees plainly assert in the Talmud that they so selected them. For in the treatise of Sabbathus, chapter ii., folio 30, page 2, it is written: R. Jehuda, surnamed Rabbi, reports that the experts wished to conceal the book of Ecclesiastes because they found therein words opposed to the law (that is, to the

18   See Endnote 23.

book of the law of Moses). Why did they not hide it? "Because it begins in accordance with the law, and ends according to the law;" and a little further on we read: "They sought also to conceal the book of Proverbs." And in the first chapter of the same treatise, fol. 13, page 2: "Verily, name one man for good, even he who was called Neghunja, the son of Hezekiah: for, save for him, the book of Ezekiel would been concealed, because it agreed not with the words of the law."

It is thus abundantly clear that men expert in the law summoned a council to decide which books should be received into the canon, and which excluded. If any man, therefore, wishes to be certified as to the authority of all the books, let him call a fresh council, and ask every member his reasons.

The time has now come for examining in the same manner the books in the New Testament; but as I learn that the task has been already performed by men highly skilled in science and languages, and as I do not myself possess a knowledge of Greek sufficiently exact for the task; lastly, as we have lost the originals of those books which were written in Hebrew, I prefer to decline the undertaking. However, I will touch on those points which have most bearing on my subject in the following chapter.

END OF PART II

Author's Endnotes to the

Theologico-Political Treatise

CHAPTERS VI TO X

CHAPTER VI

Endnote 6.   We doubt of the existence of God, and consequently of all else, so long as we have no clear and distinct
idea of God, but only a confused one. For as he who knows
not rightly the nature of a triangle, knows not that its three
angles are equal to two right angles, so he who conceives the
Divine nature confusedly, does not see that it pertains to the
nature of God to exist. Now, to conceive the nature of God
clearly and distinctly, it is necessary to pay attention to a certain number of very simple notions, called general notions,
and by their help to associate the conceptions which we form
of the attributes of the Divine nature. It then, for the first
time, becomes clear to us, that God exists necessarily, that
He is omnipresent, and that all our conceptions involve in
themselves the nature of God and are conceived through it.
Lastly, we see that all our adequate ideas are true. Compare
on this point the prolegomena to book, "Principles of Des-
cartes's philosophy set forth geometrically."

CHAPTER VII

Endnote 7.   "It is impossible to find a method which would enable us to gain a certain knowledge of all the statements in Scripture." I mean impossible for us who have not the habitual use of the
language, and have lost the precise meaning of its phraseology.

Endnote 8. "Not in things whereof the understanding can gain a clear and distinct idea, and which are conceivable through themselves." By things conceivable I mean not only those which are rigidly proved, but also those whereof we are morally certain, and are wont to hear without wonder, though they are incapable of proof. Everyone can see the truth of Euclid's propositions before they are proved. So also the histories of things both future and past which do not surpass human credence, laws, institutions, manners, I call conceivable and clear, though they cannot be proved mathematically. But hieroglyphics and histories which seem to pass the bounds of belief I call inconceivable; yet even among these last there are many which our method enables us to investigate, and to discover the meaning of their narrator.

CHAPTER VIII

Endnote 9. "Mount Moriah is called the mount of God." That is by the historian, not by Abraham, for he says that the place now called "In the mount of the Lord it shall be revealed," was called by Abraham, "the Lord shall provide."

Endnote 10. "Before that territory (Idumoea) was conquered by David." From this time to the reign of Jehoram when they again separated from the Jewish kingdom (2 Kings viii:20), the Idumaeans had no king, princes appointed by the Jews supplied the place of kings (1 Kings xxii:48), in fact the prince of Idumaea is called a king (2 Kings iii:9).

It may be doubted whether the last of the Idumaean kings had begun to reign before the accession of Saul, or whether Scripture in this chapter of Genesis wished to enumerate only such kings as were independent. It is evidently mere trifling to wish to enrol among Hebrew kings the name of Moses, who set up a dominion entirely different from a monarchy.

CHAPTER IX

Endnote 11. "With few exceptions." One of these exceptions is found in 2 Kings xviii:20, where we read, "Thou sayest (but they are but vain words)," the second person being used. In Isaiah xxxvi:5, we read "I say (but they are but vain words) I have counsel and strength for war," and in the twenty-second verse of the chapter in Kings it is written, "But if ye say," the plural number being used, whereas Isaiah gives the singular. The text in Isaiah does not contain the words found in 2 Kings xxxii:32. Thus there are several cases of various readings where it is impossible to distinguish the best.

Endnote 12. "The expressions in the two passages are so varied." For instance we read in 2 Sam. vii:6, "But I have walked in a tent and in a tabernacle." Whereas in 1 Chron. xvii:5, "but have gone from tent to tent and from one tabernacle to another." In 2 Sam. vii:10, we read, "to afflict them," whereas in 1 Chron. vii:9, we find a different expression. I could point out other differences still greater, but a single reading of the chapters in question will suffice to make them manifest to all who are neither blind nor devoid of sense.

Endnote 13. "This time cannot refer to what immediately precedes." It is plain from the context that this passage must allude to the time when Joseph was sold by his brethren. But this is not all. We may draw the same conclusion from the age of Judah, who was than twenty-two years old at most, taking as basis of calculation his own history just narrated. It follows, indeed, from the last verse of Gen. xxx., that Judah was born in the tenth of the years of Jacob's servitude to Laban, and Joseph in the fourteenth. Now, as we know that Joseph was seventeen years old when sold by his brethren, Judah was then not more than twenty-one. Hence, those writers who assert that Judah's long absence from his father's house took place before Joseph was sold, only seek to delude themselves and to call in question the Scriptural authority which they are anxious to protect.

Endnote 14. "Dinah was scarcely seven years old when she was violated by Schechem." The opinion held by some that Jacob wandered about eight or ten years between Mesopotamia and Bethel, savours of the ridiculous; if respect for Aben Ezra, allows me to say so. For it is clear that Jacob had two reasons for haste: first, the desire to see his old parents; secondly, and chiefly to perform, the vow made when he fled from his brother (Gen. xxviii:10 and xxxi:13, and xxxv:1). We read (Gen. xxxi:3), that God had commanded him to fulfill his vow, and promised him help for returning to his country. If these considerations seem conjectures rather than reasons, I will waive the point and admit that Jacob, more unfortunate than Ulysses, spent eight or ten years or even longer, in this short journey. At any rate it cannot be denied that Benjamin was born in the last year of this wandering, that is by the reckoning of the objectors, when Joseph was sixteen or seventeen years old, for Jacob left Laban seven years after Joseph's birth. Now from the seventeenth year of Joseph's age till the patriarch went into Egypt, not more than twenty-two years elapsed, as we have shown in this chapter. Consequently Benjamin, at the time of the journey to Egypt, was twenty-three or twenty-four at the most. He would therefore have been a grandfather in the flower of his age (Gen. xlvi:21, cf. Numb. xxvi:38, 40, and 1 Chron. viii;1), for it is certain that Bela, Benjamin's eldest son, had at that time, two sons, Addai and Naa-man. This is just as absurd as the statement that Dinah was violated at the age of seven, not to mention other impossibilities which would result from the truth of the narrative. Thus we see that unskillful endeavours to solve difficulties, only raise fresh ones, and make confusion worse confounded.

Endnote 15. "Othniel, son of Kenag, was judge for forty years." Rabbi Levi Ben Gerson and others believe that these forty years which the Bible says were passed in freedom, should be counted from the death of Joshua, and consequently include the eight years during which the people were subject to Kushan Rishathaim, while the following eighteen years must be added on to the eighty years of Ehud's and Shamgar's judgeships. In this case it would be necessary to reckon the other years of subjection among those said by the Bible to have been passed in freedom. But the Bible expressly notes the number of years of subjection, and the number of years of freedom, and further declares (Judges ii:18) that the Hebrew state was prosperous during the whole time of the judges. Therefore it is evident that Levi Ben Gerson (certainly a very learned man), and those who follow him, correct rather than interpret the Scriptures.

The same fault is committed by those who assert, that Scripture, by this general calculation of years, only intended to mark the period of the regular administration of the Hebrew state, leaving out the years of anarchy and subjection as periods of misfortune and interregnum. Scripture certainly passes over in silence periods of anarchy, but does not, as they dream, refuse to reckon them or wipe them out of the country's annals. It is clear that Ezra, in 1 Kings vi., wished to reckon absolutely all the years since the flight from Egypt. This is so plain, that no one versed in the Scriptures can doubt it. For, without going back to the precise words of the text, we may see that the genealogy of David given at the end of the book of Ruth, and I Chron. ii., scarcely accounts for so great a number of years. For Nahshon, who was prince of the tribe of Judah (Numb. vii;11), two years after the Exodus, died in the desert, and his son Salmon passed the Jordan with Joshua. Now this Salmon, according to the genealogy, was David's great-grandfather. Deducting, then, from the total of 480 years, four years for Solomon's reign, seventy for David's life, and forty for the time passed in the desert, we find that David was born 366 years after the passage of the Jordan. Hence we must believe that David's father, grandfather, great-grandfather, and great-great-grandfather begat children when they were ninety years old.

Endnote 16.   "Samson was judge for twenty years." Samson was born after the Hebrews had fallen under the dominion of the Philistines.

Endnote 17.   Otherwise, they rather correct than explain Scripture.

Endnote 18. "Kirjath-jearim." Kirjath-jearim is also called Baale of Judah. Hence Kimchi and others think that the words Baale Judah, which I have translated "the people of Judah," are the name of a town. But this is not so, for the word Baale is in the plural. Moreover, comparing this text in Samuel with I Chron. Xiii:5, we find that David did not rise up and go forth out of Baale, but that he went thither. If the author of the book of Samuel had meant to name the place whence David took the ark, he would, if he spoke Hebrew correctly, have said, "David rose up, and set forth from Baale Judah, and took the ark from thence."

CHAPTER X

Endnote 19. "After the restoration of the Temple by Judas Maccaboeus." This conjecture, if such it be, is founded on the genealogy of King Jeconiah, given in 1 Chron. iii., which finishes at the sons of Elioenai, the thirteenth in direct descent from him: whereon we must observe that Jeconiah, before his captivity, had no children; but it is probable that he had two while he was in prison, if we may draw any inference from the names he gave them. As to his grandchildren, it is evident that they were born after his deliverance, if the names be any guide, for his grandson, Pedaiah (a name meaning God hath delivered me), who, according to this chapter, was the father of Zerubbabel, was born in the thirty-seventh or thirty-eighth year of Jeconiah's life, that is thirty-three years before the restoration of liberty to the Jews by Cyrus. Therefore Zerubbabel, to whom Cyrus gave the principality of Judaea, was thirteen or fourteen years old. But we need not carry the inquiry so far: we need only read attentively the chapter of 1 Chron., already quoted, where (v. 17, sqq.) mention is made of all the posterity of Jeconiah, and compare it with the Septuagint version to see clearly that these books were not published, till after Maccabaeus had restored the Temple, the sceptre no longer belonging to the house of Jeconiah.

Endnote 20. "Zedekiah should be taken to Babylon." No one could then have suspected that the prophecy of Ezekiel contradicted that of Jeremiah, but the suspicion occurs to everyone who reads the narrative of Josephus. The event proved that both prophets were in the right.

Endnote 21. "And who wrote Nehemiah." That the greater part of the book of Nehemiah was taken from the work composed by the prophet Nehemiah himself, follows from the testimony of its author. (See chap. i.). But it is obvious that the whole of the passage contained between chap. viii. and chap. xii. verse 26, together with the two last verses of chap. xii., which form a sort of parenthesis to Nehemiah's words, were added by the historian himself, who outlived Nehemiah.

Endnote 22. "I suppose no one thinks" that Ezra was the uncle of the first high priest, named Joshua (see Ezra vii., and 1 Chron. vi:14), and went to Jerusalem from Babylon with Zerubbabel (see Nehemiah xii:1). But it appears that when he saw, that the Jews were in a state of anarchy, he returned to Babylon, as also did others (Nehem. i;2), and remained there till the reign of Artaxerxes, when his requests were granted and he went a second time to Jerusalem. Nehemiah also went to Jerusalem with Zerubbabel in the time of Cyrus (Ezra ii:2 and 63, cf. x:9, and Nehemiah x:1). The version given of the Hebrew word, translated "ambassador," is not supported by any authority, while it is certain that fresh names were given to those Jews who frequented the court. Thus Daniel was named Balteshazzar, and Zerubbabel Sheshbazzar (Dan. i:7). Nehemiah was called Atirsata, while in virtue of his office he was styled governor, or president. (Nehem. v. 24, xii:26.)

Endnote 23. "Before the time of the Maccabees there was no canon of sacred books." The synagogue styled "the great" did not begin before the subjugation of Asia by the Macedonians. The contention of Maimonides, Rabbi Abraham, Ben-David, and others, that the presidents of this synagogue were Ezra, Daniel, Nehemiah, Haggai, Zechariah, &c., is a pure fiction, resting only on rabbinical tradition. Indeed they assert that the dominion of the Persians only lasted thirty-four years, and this is their chief reason for maintaining that the decrees of the "great synagogue," or synod (rejected by the Sadducees, but accepted by the Pharisees) were ratified by the prophets, who received them from former prophets, and so in direct succession from Moses, who received them from God Himself. Such is the doctrine which the Pharisees maintain with their wonted obstinacy. Enlightened persons, however, who know the reasons for the convoking of councils, or synods, and are no strangers to the differences between Pharisees and Sadducees, can easily divine the causes which led to the assembling of this great synagogue. It is very certain that no prophet was there present, and that the decrees of the Pharisees, which they style their traditions, derive all their authority from it.

End of Endnotes to PART II.